"Rosemarie Rossetti's new book provides an immensely valuable guide and toolkit for anyone interested in applying Universal Design principles within their own homes—new or remodeled. For years, I've been looking for a tool like this one, that is not all just rules and dimensions, but that actually gives a view into the way that Universal Design can change lives, making the home a friend that supports life, as it is supposed to be, rather than an obstacle to living fully. Through her own story of suddenly changed mobility, she describes the search for solutions and the dramatic and truly stellar result of her efforts. She eloquently shares that journey, and the expertise that she's garnered along the way—an expertise now accessible to all.

Sometimes life hands us a challenge that we fear may engulf us, even crush us. But when we use that challenge instead to learn more about life and ourselves, and then share that knowledge with others, everyone benefits beyond all expectation or imagining. Rosemarie's life challenge has become that kind of lens that brings real understanding to the world of Universal Design. I will be using this book and toolkit for many years to come, as I hope you will also. If you are looking for that one book that explains this important but often misunderstood subject, this is it."

Sarah Susanka, FAIA
Architect and Author of **The Not So Big House** series, and **The Not So Big Life**
Raleigh, North Carolina

"This book takes the reader on Rosemarie Rossetti's amazing and inspiring personal and professional journey leading ultimately to the creation of her Universal Design Living Laboratory (UDLL). The UDLL is both a home for she and her husband Mark, as well as a demonstration site.

The book chronicles the process of designing the home, selecting products, managing construction, and its evolution into the place it is now. There are lessons here for anyone who is embarking on a home design/build process.

The home has much to recommend. It nicely displays numerous generic UD features that everyone can take advantage of, virtually every day: graded, step-free entrance; gracious open-plan interior; curbless shower; level exit back patio; hand held shower; lever door handles; raised outlets; lowered wall controls; front control appliances; elevator; home technology; and many more. These features are highly marketable to mainstream home buyers. While not all the product selections are low-cost, the basic functionality of the home can be adapted to almost any budget.

TESTIMONIALS

The home demonstrates how UD homes benefit everyone every day and REALLY benefits us at certain points in our lives or those of us with certain life circumstances. Because, not only does the house showcase great UD, it also shows what you can do if you need to add custom features for example, lowered kitchen work surfaces with kneespace for seated users.

The Toolkit has cost information, and extensive checklists and resources listings. This is a very useful book for anyone who is thinking about designing and building differently, or who is wondering what type of features they might like to include in their next home."

Richard Duncan
Executive Director - The R.L. Mace Universal Design Institute
Ashville, North Carolina

"The Universal Design Living Laboratory Toolkit is a "must have and must use" book to better educate yourself about how to understand universal design practices and techniques and how to apply them to your residential, commercial, retail, resort, recreational, institutional and governmental environments!

You'll have a plethora of practical application, educational and direct resources that you can use with confidence today!"

S. Robert August, BA, MIM, NAHB Life Director, Fellow, MIRM, CMP, CSP, MCSP, CAASH
President - North Star Synergies, Inc.
Centennial, Colorado

"The Universal Design Toolkit" offers designers, laypersons, and others comprehensive information about universal design. It debunks the myths about universal design, and provides detailed information on design requirements, funding sources, finding a qualified design professional, and questions designers and clients should ask, cost estimates and much more. Because universal design improves life for everyone, any person thinking of renting, buying, building, or remodeling a house will find much useful information in this book."

Jack L. Nasar, Emeritus Professor City & Regional Planning
Academy Professor, Emeritus Academy
The Ohio State University
Columbus, Ohio

"First and foremost, The Universal Design Toolkit is a love story between two individuals who risked turning a life-altering experience into a mission to make a difference. This is a book about resilience, contribution, and how to live fully—not in spite of limitations, but because of them.

The book begins with Rosemarie's accident, but it is not the focus, rather it provides context for the journey to The Universal Design Living Laboratory; a showcase for those who seek the best practices in human-centered design and accessibility solutions for all.

This is hands-down the most comprehensive work on Universal Design I have read. It is written from an end-user's point of view, so emphasis on practicality.

For all of us who will benefit from this work, we should be forever grateful that Rosemarie and Mark took to heart the theme: "Failure is not an option.""

Patrick J. Roden, Ph.D.
aginginplace.com
Portland, Oregon

"The Universal Design Toolkit is the "bible" for anyone interested in design, construction, or sales for the rapidly growing Universal Design industry. The advice, tips and suggestions provided will help architects, building developers, realtors, interior designers and other professionals can take years off their experiential learning curve. Thanks to Rosemarie Rossetti, PhD for creating this incredibly valuable resource."

Rosalind Sedacca, CCT
Marketing Consultant
Boynton Beach, Florida

"The Universal Design Toolkit is a wonderful tool to add to your tool belt. Rosemarie's inspiring story serves as a catalyst to this wonderful book. More than numbers and measurements, Rosemarie puts the individual in the picture with an approach to make universal design accessible for everyone. A must have resource for professionals, students, individuals, and families who are interested in making their homes and our world a more accessible place."

Dennis Cleary, MS, OTD, OTR/L
Assistant Professor of Occupational Therapy
The Ohio State University
Columbus, Ohio

TESTIMONIALS

"The Universal Design Toolkit is a very useful and comprehensive manual for anyone interested in the concept of Universal Design. The author Rosemarie Rossetti, is passionate about the topic since she has lived through events that require UD concepts in her home. She has educated herself on UD, compiled extensive resources, and written the book so it is not just a cookbook to introduce UD, but a heartfelt narrative on one person's personal story. I think the book has a place for anyone working in the field of UD such as REALTORS®, CAPS specialists, architects, builders, and developers, and anyone that has the ability to help people live in an environment that has no barriers to the people living there. I highly recommend this book."

John D. Frenzel, REALTOR®
Long Term Care Specialist
Campbell, California

"This is an educational "must read" for any and all professionals and consumers interested in developing a qualified knowledge base for universal design living. This book will be your compass from start to finish in universal design from the selecting of an architect, builder or remodeler up to and including all of the important questions to ask, universal design features and safety checklists, trade reference resources and much more comprehensive application information.

Our direct communications with Rosemarie and husband, Mark during our home design was nothing short of amazing and truly invaluable. As consultants, their first hand knowledge and experience with their own Universal Design Living Laboratory (UDLL) provided us with everything we needed to move confidently into the future with our own universally designed home. The "Universal Design Toolkit" is for everybody and will provide any individual or trade professional a greater understanding of the principles behind this exciting, future now lifestyle."

Victoria & Rich Parsons
Parker, Colorado

"Universal Design Toolkit is an invaluable guide to making homes accessible. From expert insights, to specifics on space design and costs, to comprehensive resource lists, it's all here."

Wendy A. Jordan
Author - *Universal Design for the Home: Great-Looking, Great-Living Design for All Ages, Abilities, and Circumstances*
Washington, D.C.

TESTIMONIALS

"Get a copy of this book and be prepared to be inspired! The book is very well organized and easy to follow. You don't know what you don't know until you've seen this book!

The Universal Design Toolkit is such a valuable source of information on practical adaptations that can be incorporated into a new or existing home. There are ideas in this book that you've never thought of and solutions to problems you thought you had to live with.

Whether you're looking for ideas to age in place or need to make adaptations to your current living space to accommodate a new disability, this book will guide you through the process.

Rosemarie and her husband Mark have done so much research on the subject. There is a practical insight that comes from living with a disability and building a home from the ground up that is so powerful.

A visitor to their beautiful home would never know that it is constructed to enable a disabled person to function independently! They have thought of everything and their home is so functional that you wonder why aren't all homes constructed like this. This book tells you how to go about making this dream come true. They've gathered all the information you need in one place.

My husband and I are retired physicians in our seventies. We recently downsized to a ranch home but it could be so much more functional for us as we age if the builder had planned ahead! This book gives you that information and knowledge is power!

I highly recommend this book!"

Carol & Pete Hostetter
Loveland, Ohio

"Rosemarie Rossetti has a commitment and passion for spreading the word regarding design that improves access, and beyond that, she has a perspective and personal experience which few can claim. Rosemarie immersed herself in all aspects of the design, building, and finishing of her home, and she shares that experience and knowledge in this book."

Mary Jo Peterson
President - Mary Jo Peterson, Inc. - Kitchen, Bath, and Universal Design
Brookfield, Connecticut

TESTIMONIALS

"This toolkit is for people dedicated to living comfortably and safely in their homes for many generations. Aside from the emotional benefits of staying in one's home, the costs out-of-home care can be more than most families can afford. Universal Design features may be incorporated into any home pre and post construction from simple grab bars in the bathrooms to entirely accessible homes. Rosemarie and Mark provide comprehensive information that will save countless hours of research and unnecessary costs."

Susan Schubert
Author - ***Caring for Challenging Relatives & Friends; There's a Human in MY Bed; Emotional Intelligence Works***, etc.
Pickerington, Ohio

"This Book is a must read. Rosemarie and Mark have lived the journey of a physical injury and have been able to achieve a living style with fewer challenges. Universal Design Living is the key to a comfortable life style within your home. This applies not only to a physical challenge but to all of us as we enter our Second Stage of Life."

Cassie Ann Reynolds
Columbus, Ohio

"While helping my sister develop a design for her new home, which was to include many universal design features, we were introduced to Rosemarie who shared many valuable tips and things we would have never considered on our own. Now, she has compiled that wealth of information into an absolute must-have resource for ANY home designer that we're glad we have on our bookshelf!"

Christy Heckel
Powell, Ohio

"Don't just learn about universal design, let yourself be inspired by the story and practical knowledge of this subject from Rosemarie Rossetti. She not only speaks and writes on this topic – but lives the benefits of design which can work for everyone from grandchildren to grandparents through her beautifully designed home!"

Mike Foti
President, Innovate Building Solutions
Cleveland, Ohio

"Rosemarie Rossetti is an inspiration! Many can talk about helping individuals who have disabilities, few can talk from experience. Rosemarie is an example of how an accident can be so dramatically life changing. We can only imagine what she has gone through, but now, through the Universal Design Toolkit, she brings shinning rays of hope and help to so many in need now and in the future.

Her process of creating an interprofessional network of experts led to improving her life, and now she shares what she has learned. We met Rosemarie, and her husband Mark, at their internationally acclaimed demonstration home, the Universal Design Living Laboratory in Columbus, Ohio. After touring their beautiful and comfortable home (but not institutional looking) and hearing the stories directly from them, especially how difficult it was to bring new ideas to the industry, we applaud them and encourage everyone to learn from Rosemarie."

Louie Delaware & Erik Listou
Co-Founders of the *Living In Place Institute* - www.LIPI.Institute
Loveland, Colorado

"Life can take unexpected detours. Rosemarie Rossetti knows exactly how unexplainable tragedy can end dreams...or begin new ones. Her story will not only inspire those who have expeienced despair but is helpful for every adult facing aging and wanting to remain at home. All readers will benefit by understanding universal design. And some application will be important to you or someone you love today or tomorrow. This is an eyeopening how-to-guide to living fully in spite of disabilities or aging."

Stan Craig
Author - *Foretalk: The 7 Critical Conversations for Living in the Season of Now*
Louisville, Kentucky

"I found your book to be a good overview of the process for people who are thinking of creating Universally Designed homes. It lays out for home owners who have little experience with the custom construction process many of the issue and areas of concern that are often involved in Universal Design projects. It can help them to understand the challenges involved in directing a team to create spaces that really work for the users."

John P.S. Salmen, FAIA
President - Universal Designers & Consultants, Inc.
Silver Spring, Maryland

TESTIMONIALS

"To incorporate universal design in senior housing, it takes time and creativity. That's why most architect's miss it. That's why we need Rosemarie Rossetti—she gets it right!"

Ken Mitchell
Ken Mitchell Senior Homes
McKinney, Texas

"This book is a page-turner!

Rosemarie Rossetti's Universal Design Toolkit contains a wealth of details and resources needed to build accessible homes. Occupational therapists and other professionals in the home building industry will find this book invaluable as a reference for Universal Design guidelines to ensure their specifications meet their client's needs.

Her book provides Universal Design features and aspects a home also needs to be visitable, and for those who wish to live in their home for a lifetime. The Universal Design Toolkit illustrates Dr. Rossetti's knowledge, passion, and commitment to making our world more accessible."

Carroll T. Fernstrom, OTR / L
Occupational Therapist, OT - Accessibility Consulting
Raleigh, North Carolina

"By sharing her knowledge in the Universal Design Toolkit Rosemarie not only sets the standard for the quintessential resource for professionals and lay persons, she also empowers the individual by improving their quality of life and helping ALL people to live with better independence and dignity."

Michael V. Sajdyk
Owner/President - Feng Shui Concepts & Designs
Indianapolis, Indiana

"Working with Rosemarie and Mark as they built their Universal Design Dream House was a great experience! The Universal Design Toolkit is a wonderful resource for anyone hoping to expand the capabilities of any home. Age in place and live in a home that nurtures you!"

Cathy Van Volkenburg, CPO®
Certified Professional Organizer - Owner, Accent on Organizing
Columbus, Ohio

"Rosemarie experienced first-hand the challenges of equal access but, more importantly, the need for designs that are inclusive of all. Her book, Universal Design Toolkit provides a resource for anyone to use."

Linda Nussbaumer, PhD, CID-MN, ASID, IDEC
Professor Emerita, South Dakota State University
Lake Crystal, Minnesota

"An exceptional body of work that gives all buyers and builders the ability to learn from real world experience. Thank you for all that you have done for our industry and for those of us who live to serve others in their personalized living needs."

Mike Davidson
Vice President Sales & Marketing - Wonderland Homes
Denver, Colorado

"Rosemarie Rossetti's story is a shining example of turning a very significant life challenge into a very positive outcome for many to benefit from. Her courage will inspire everyone who comes to know her through her writing, speaking and her actions."

Gerry Murak
Author - *Our Fathers Who Art in Heaven...And What They Continue to Teach Us*
Getzville, NY

UNIVERSAL DESIGN TOOLKIT

Rosemarie Rossetti, Ph.D.

UNIVERSAL DESIGN TOOLKIT

Copyright © MMXVII by Rosemarie Rossetti, Ph.D.

All rights reserved. No part of this book may be reproduced by any mechanical, photographic, or electronic process, or in the form of a phonographic recording; nor may it be stored in a retrieval system, transmitted, or otherwise be copied for public or private use – other than for "fair use" as brief quotations embodied in articles and reviews without prior written permission of the author.

ISBN Number (print):

978-0-9988287-3-2

Rosemarie@udll.com

http://www.udll.com

PUBLISHED BY ROSSETTI ENTERPRISES INC.

Rosemarie@RosemarieSpeaks.com

http://www.RosemarieSpeaks.com

Phone: 614.471.6100

First Edition

Disclaimer

This toolkit is designed to provide information, motivation and educational concepts and ideas to our readers. This toolkit is sold with the understanding that we are not promoting, warranting or otherwise advocating any ideas, advice or solutions as being suitable for a particular purpose or a particular design. In addition, we are not endorsing any products, organizations, corporations or other entities that are mentioned in the toolkit. Use the information provided to assist you but do not rely solely on this information when making decisions or design plans. You should get professional opinions on your use of any information contained in this toolkit. Thank you for purchasing our toolkit.

Cover and layout design by Mark Leder,
based on a concept from Mohammad Alauddin
Edited by Mark Leder

Unless otherwise acknowledged, all photography by Mark Leder

CONTENTS

	Foreword by E.J. Thomas	19
	The Story Behind the Universal Design Living Laboratory	21
	Introduction	59
CHAPTER 1:	Benefits of Having Universal Design Features in Homes	67
CHAPTER 2:	The Principles of Universal Design	73
CHAPTER 3:	Ten Myths About Universal Design	79
CHAPTER 4:	Glossary of Terms Related to Universal Design	85
CHAPTER 5:	Important Space Planning Dimensions for People Who Use Wheelchairs or Walkers	89
CHAPTER 6:	Professionals: Questions to Ask Your Clients about their Current and Future Needs	121
CHAPTER 7:	Sources of Funding to Repair, Modify, Remodel or Build a New Universal Design Home	123
CHAPTER 8:	How to Find a Professional Who is Knowledgeable about Universal Design (Architect, Home Designer, Builder, Remodeler, Interior Designer, Lighting Designer, Occupational Therapist, Landscape Designer and Realtor)	143

CONTENTS

CHAPTER 9:	Consumers: Questions to Ask When Selecting a Designer and Builder/Remodeler	151
CHAPTER 10:	How to Find House Plans, Floor Plans and Room Designs for Universal Design Homes	155
CHAPTER 11:	Estimated Construction and Product Costs for Selected Universal Design Features	159
CHAPTER 12:	Universal Design Features Checklist by Room at the Universal Design Living Laboratory	163
CHAPTER 13:	Universal Design Checklists, Safety Checklists, Home Assessments, and Certification Programs	173
CHAPTER 14:	Survey Finds Homebuyers Needs for Accessible Housing are Unmet	187
CHAPTER 15:	Perceived Value of Visitable Housing in Ohio	191
CHAPTER 16:	Resources	195
	About Rosemarie Rossetti, Ph.D.	205
	Putting Universal Design to Work for You	209
	Order More Copies of the Universal Design Toolkit	211

Rosemarie's story is one of pluck and determination in the face of personal tragedy. She has chosen to turn personal challenge into an individualized approach that, embraced by architects and builders in the years to come, has the potential of providing countless individuals with a productive, independent and satisfying home life. It is an honor to share my personal remarks about the book she's written, one that illustrates the product of much thought and dedication.

About a year ago I had the opportunity to visit the Rossetti home with members of our construction team to view how their home design has shattered the many myths associated with the notion of "Universal Design." Truly inspirational, its layout and functionality demonstrated in room after room how a home can be crafted to serve its occupants, whether fully functional or physically impaired.

This book is a reflection of the many hours, spanning a number of years, which were invested in developing a concept that is as beautiful as it is functional for its occupants. As such, I commend it to the reader's study and application for the development and construction of homes that, in the future, will allow anyone physically challenged to live with dignity and self-sufficiency.

E.J. Thomas, President & CEO
Habitat for Humanity-MidOhio
Columbus, Ohio

FOREWARD

THE STORY BEHIND THE UNIVERSAL DESIGN LIVING LABORATORY

On June 13, 1998 my husband, Mark Leder, and I decided to celebrate our third wedding anniversary by going on a bicycle ride. It was a beautiful day with a clear blue sky — perfect biking weather. I was riding along the path ahead of Mark, when he heard a loud noise and yelled, "*Look over there something is falling!* **STOP!**" Suddenly a 7,000 pound tree came crashing down on me, leaving me unconscious on the bike path. My life was changed in that instant! I was paralyzed from the waist down with a spinal cord injury.

In the days following the injury and emergency surgery, I lay in the hospital angry, very scared and really mad at the world. My life was catastrophically disrupted and changed. I could not see myself living with this loss. I was in constant pain. My legs wouldn't move. I couldn't even turn in bed. My hands were so paralyzed that Mark had to feed me.

I saw my life as wasted! Everything that I had accomplished in my life was a waste! My eight years of college and Ph.D. were wasted! *How am I going to survive? How are my two businesses going to survive?*

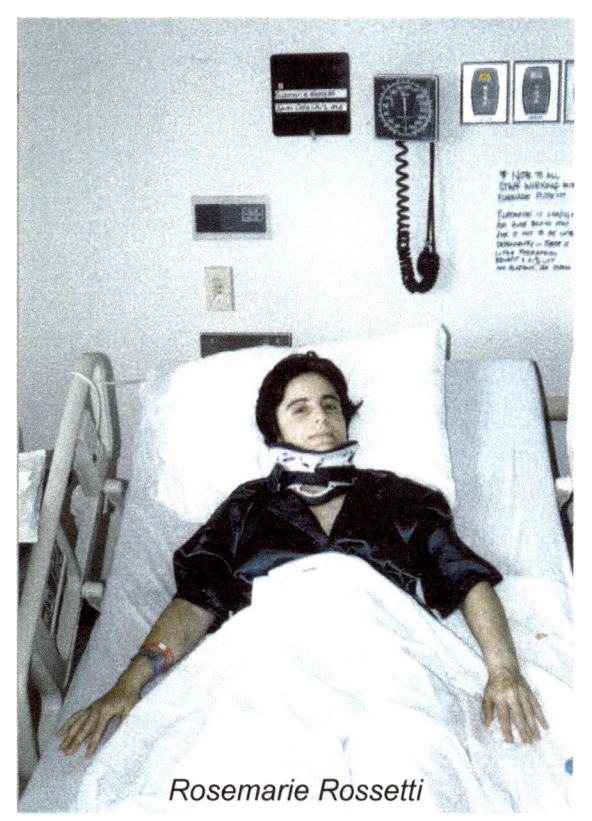
Rosemarie Rossetti

 Universal Design Toolkit

My marriage, my two businesses and my finances are in jeopardy. I could lose Mark, our house, everything!

I cried over the things I thought I would never be able to do again, things that I had enjoyed before my injury. Mark and I found togetherness in our recreational activities. We not only loved to ride our bikes, but we loved to ski, hike, dance, and play racquetball.

I looked deep within myself and found new resolve and new strength to attempt to rebuild my life. I had a lot invested in my life to this point in time, and I wasn't about to lose the momentum that years of hard work had provided, including the income from my two businesses. I had a Ph.D. with eight years of college behind me. I had a great husband that I didn't want to lose.

I used the resources that I had available to me during my rehabilitation. At the Dodd Hall rehabilitation center at The Ohio State University Wexner Medical Center, I told my physical therapist "I am willing to work and do anything you say. I want my life back and I will do whatever you tell me". I wanted a full recovery. I wanted the pain to go away. I wanted to be able to do things for myself again and someday walk.

Every day I pushed myself harder. I was determined to regain the most basic of life skills; feeding myself, grooming, moving in bed, sitting up, pushing myself in a wheelchair.

Coming Home from the Hospital - Frustrations Build

After six weeks of inpatient rehabilitation (which seemed like an eternity), I finally went home on July 21, 1998 to attempt to rebuild my life. Mark transferred me from his car and into my wheelchair, and pushed me up a steep temporary wooden ramp to the front door of our two-story home. I went into my home for the first time as a wheelchair user. This was a rude awakening!

Universal Design Toolkit

I sat in the foyer in my manual wheelchair and slowly gazed around the house. I was wearing a neck and body brace. Because of my injury, I was transformed from a previously active standing height of 5'-1" to a permanently seated 4'-2" in my wheelchair. I made the attempt to roll myself into the carpeted great room and discovered I was too weak. Padding underneath the carpet made it all the more fatiguing. Mark had to push me across the carpet into the kitchen where I could roll on the linoleum floor.

I quickly realized how disabling my home was to me.

- Fifty percent of my home was now inaccessible.
- Stairs prevented me from using the basement or second floor.
- Many room doorways were too narrow to fit through.
- I couldn't go out the back door and down the steps into my backyard garden.

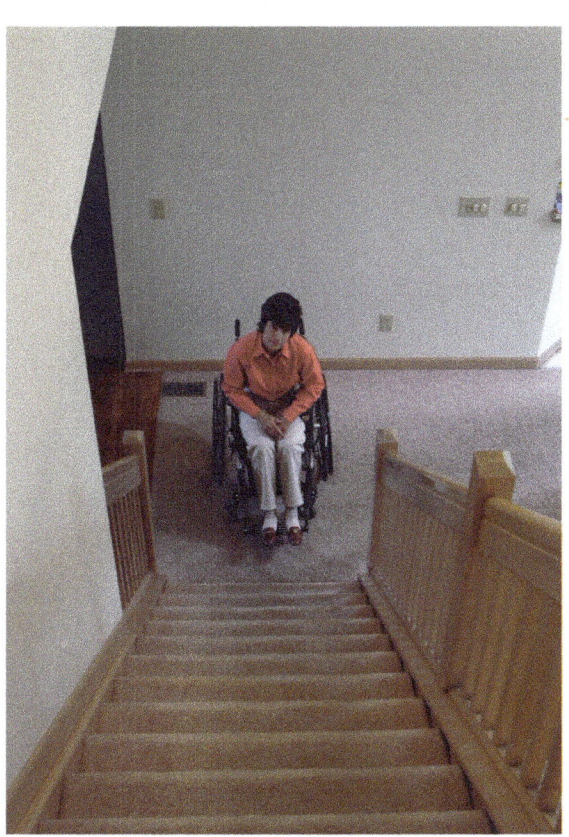

- In the kitchen, I couldn't reach items in the wall cabinets, not even a glass to get a drink of water.
- I couldn't reach the water faucet at the sink.
- I couldn't enter many of the closets because the doorways were too narrow.
- I couldn't reach clothing rods and shelves in the closet.
- I couldn't turn around in the hallways because they were too narrow.

THE STORY

Universal Design Toolkit

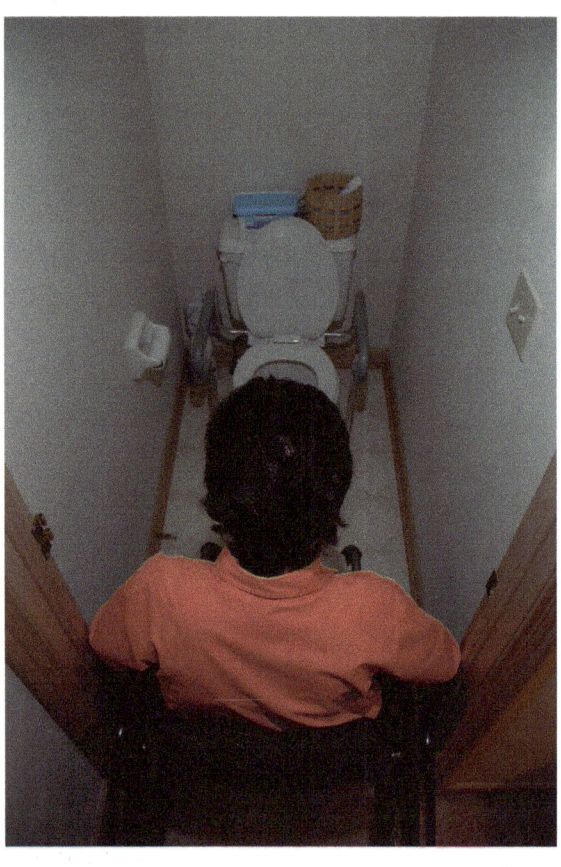

- I couldn't use the bathroom toilet area, because I couldn't get in. A door had to be removed, but I lost my privacy.

- I couldn't use my bathtub

- The towel bars were out of my reach.

I struggled to be independent again and do things for myself. Everywhere I turned there were frustrating barriers, obstacles and limitations. I was handicapped by my spinal cord injury and now my home intensified my disability. Our dream home had turned into a nightmare!

Because of my disability I needed lots of help with daily living skills like getting out of bed, taking a shower, getting dressed, toileting, cooking, and getting around in our home. After three years of marriage, Mark was now thrust into the unfamiliar position of being my main caregiver, nurse, and housekeeper during the times he was not working. He got me out of bed each morning. He dressed me and helped me with my personal hygiene. He did the laundry, bought the groceries, did the cooking, yard work, and cleaned our home. He tried to console me but he couldn't even hold my hand without causing me pain, due to my injury. He tried to make me feel like his wife instead of his patient.

When I arrived home from the rehabilitation center in July of 1998, I hired Youlandia Peake to be my caregiver when Mark was at work. She assisted me with all daily living skills, transported me to and from my outpatient physical and occupational therapy three days a week, took me to doctor's appointments, cleaned the house, did the laundry, and cooked meals. She worked for me until May 1999 when I was finally able to independently drive a wheelchair accessible modified van.

Universal Design Toolkit

Mark and I wondered how permanent my injury would be and if I would ever be walking again. My doctor told me that walking again with braces on my legs and arm crutches was possible and that most of my recovery would occur in the first two years. We didn't want to remodel our home to accommodate my needs too quickly, should there be an outside chance that I would be walking in a few years.

I continued to hope that someday we would find another house that would work better for me — where I would have things within reach. A home that was more comfortable and safe, providing me an independent lifestyle. A place where I would not be dependent on my husband to retrieve items which were not accessible.

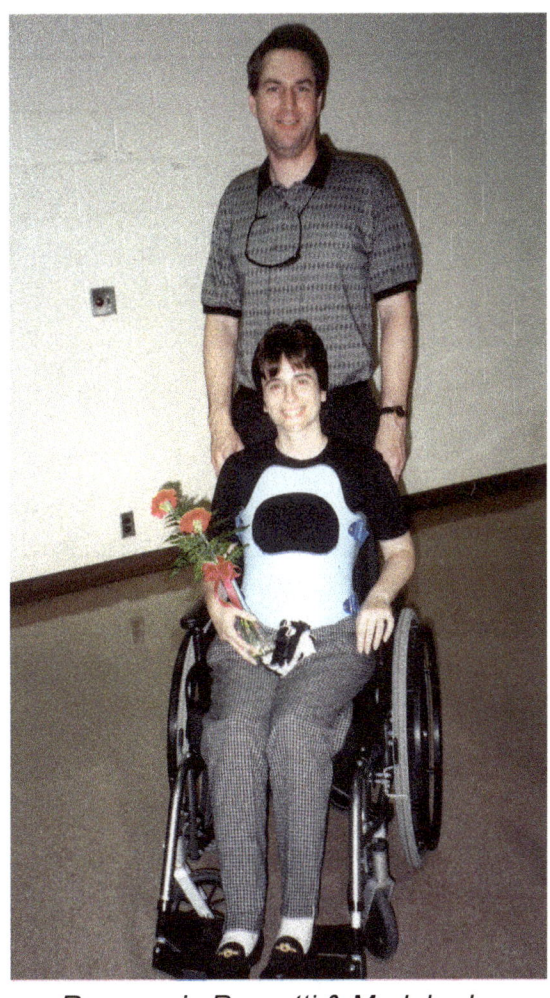
Rosemarie Rossetti & Mark Leder

With little money to invest, we worked with what we had to make changes and modifications. The temporary steep wooden ramp at the front door was replaced by an electric platform lift at the front porch. The porch surface was raised to provide a level surface from the platform lift to the interior of our home. This was paid for by the Ohio Bureau of Vocational Rehabilitation. Doors were removed in the bathroom and on the shower, to allow me access. Grab bars were installed in the toileting areas. Cabinet and pantry contents had to be repositioned to facilitate access to the most critically needed items. Full extension drawers were installed in the lower kitchen cabinets. Long handled reaching devices were placed in every room which gave me the ability to retrieve the clothes from the washer, reach food in the pantry, and grab hanging and folded clothing in closets.

THE STORY

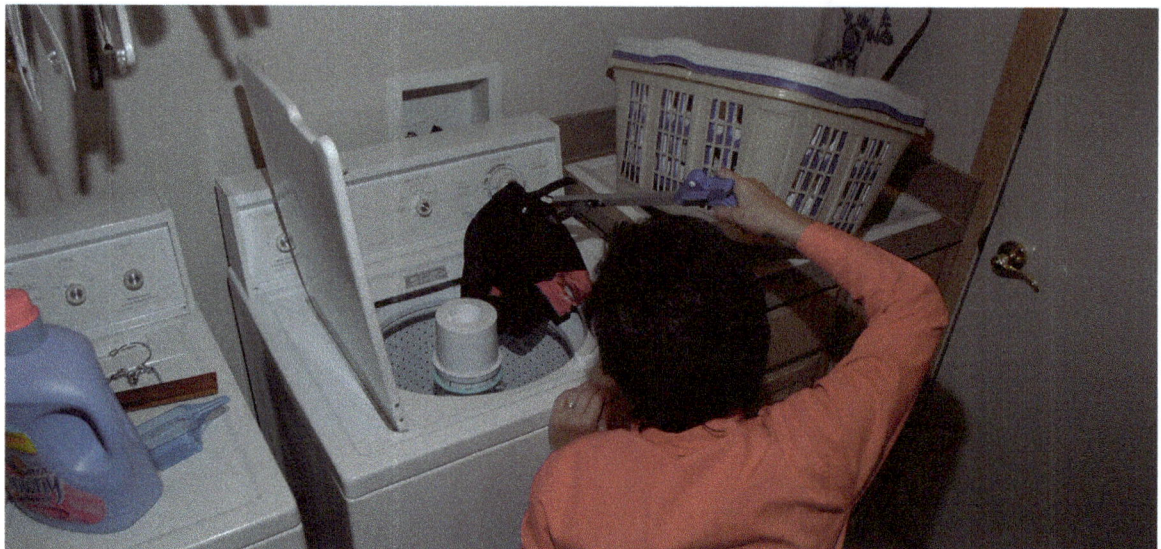

The laundry room, next to the garage entryway, was too tiny to maneuver in my wheelchair. I would get angry just trying to get into this room. The door to the laundry room was removed to give me a little more space, but still I struggled and scratched the washer and dryer with the footrest on my wheelchair. I couldn't reach into the top loading washer to remove the wet clothes. It was hard to reposition my wheelchair to take the wet clothes and put them in the front loading dryer. It took me forever to do a load of laundry!

Although these home modifications helped to improve the quality of my life, problems still existed. I couldn't go down the steps into the garage to get into my van. I had to go out the front door, down the electric platform lift and around the front walk. When I brought home

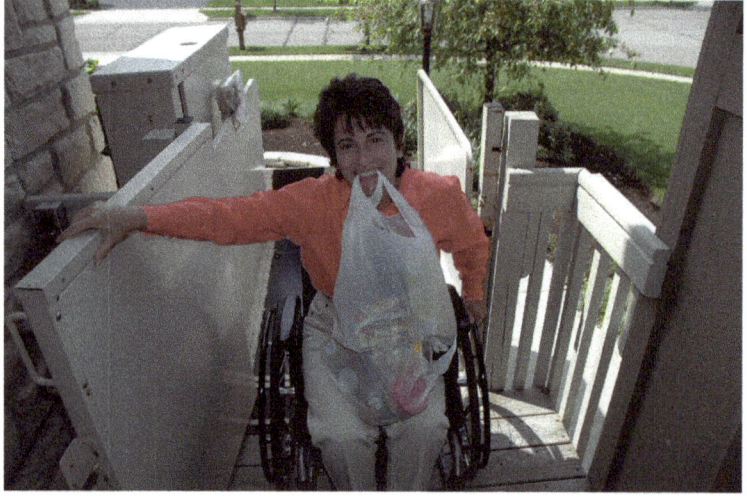

groceries I had to carry the bags in my mouth while I maneuvered across the walk and up the electric platform lift. Even getting something out of my freezer in the garage required a trip out the front door.

THE STORY

 Universal Design Toolkit

I'm a professional speaker, writer, publisher and consultant who works from home. My first floor office space for my business was a cramped 11' X 11'. I needed space to work and access to my desk, computer, files, books, phone, fax, printer and stored materials. Many of my files and resources, as well as book inventory and marketing materials for my publishing company were stored in the basement. These items were only accessible to me upon my request to Mark to bring these items upstairs.

Rebuilding my life was a slow process. Three days a week for the first two years after my injury, I went to physical and occupational therapy as an outpatient at The Ohio State University Wexner Medical Center. I worked to regain the strength necessary to take care of my daily personal needs. A red-letter day occurred when I was able to tie my shoes.

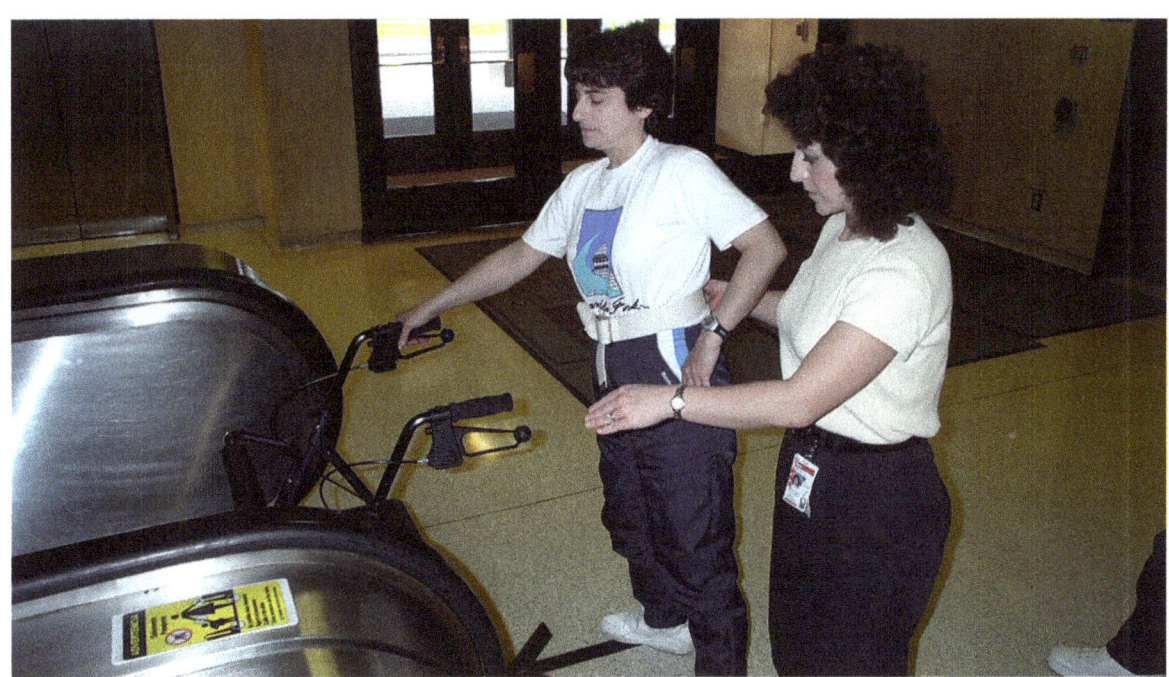
Rosemarie Rossetti assisted by Diane Brown, Physical Therapist, The Ohio State University

I began to rebuild my business and started speaking and writing again. I took lessons in adaptive skiing and wheelchair dancing. In 2000, Mark and I each bought a three wheeled recumbent bicycle and started to ride the trails again. Life balance was being restored.

Universal Design Toolkit

THE STORY

 Universal Design Toolkit

In Search for a Home

After five years of living in our home in a state of frustration after my injury, Mark and I realized that our home, that we had built and moved into in the fall of 1995, would never fully meet my need for independence, mobility, safety, comfort and convenience.

Mark and I talked about what would need to be done to remodel it. We determined that the home would require drastic reconfigurations, costing more than the home's value. The expense would not be worth the investment. We would have had to install an elevator, remodel and enlarge the kitchen and bathrooms, and would still have the platform lift at our front door, the only accessible entrance.

One day in 2003, we had a serious discussion as we drove around looking at homes for sale. We concluded that the time had come to sell our home and look for something to better suit our needs.

We did not have additional funds available to go beyond the value of our existing home. We were fortunate to have a great location, substantial equity in the home, and a strong market that increased valuations in our neighborhood.

In the summer of 2004, we contacted a Realtor and researched what existing homes were on the market. After several viewings, none of them had the accessibility features I needed.

We toured new model homes all over the Columbus, Ohio area in search of a floor plan and a lot to build a new home. These model homes were not wheelchair accessible, so Mark had to pull me up the steps in the garage or at the front door in my wheelchair. Sometimes the sales offices weren't accessible, so again Mark had to come to my aid just to get into the door. We interviewed builders and reviewed floor plans. No accessible features were included in these models and few options were presented to us by the builders. Builders had only a few ranch-style floor plans available. I became very discouraged by the prospect of living in a home that frustrated and limited me.

Mark said, "Why can't anybody understand this, why don't they think this through and make homes accessible for everyone? Why are all these homes the same, without features that would accommodate people in wheelchairs? Why are all the homes two stories?"

We both wondered why builders weren't incorporating accessibility into their existing floor plans. Why weren't these features and benefits discussed with home buyers to identify their current and future needs?

Discovering Universal Design

I first learned about universal design when reading a magazine article and seeing a photo of a woman in a wheelchair in her universal design kitchen. That article gave Mark and me hope, and the idea that we could have a new home where life would once again be fully functional for me.

We learned that universal design is a framework for the design of living and working spaces and products, benefiting the widest possible range of people in the widest range of situations without special or separate design. Universal design is human-centered design, accommodating people of all sizes, ages, and abilities.

A home designed with universal design principles certainly makes life easier, not only for those with mobility limitations, but also for those who are young, old, short or tall. We are a good couple to illustrate the need for universal design, as Mark stands at 6'4" and I am 4'2" tall seated in my wheelchair. Universal design is for everyone and the integrated features blend in seamlessly in the home design. Universal design need not look institutional, but rather can be done beautifully.

Universal design features can be included in homes, regardless of the house size or price of the home. For example Habitat for Humanity builds small homes for low-income families and includes many universal design features to assure that the homes accommodate people who use wheelchairs.

Universal Design Toolkit

Universal design features enable the occupants to age in place if they choose. This gives families options rather than being forced to move.

Imagine having a home that accommodates a person during the time of a temporary or a permanent illness or disability. The cost of staying home and having in-home caregiving by family members or paid staff is considerably more affordable than living in an assisted living facility. Due to the features of universal design that support safety and accessibility throughout a person's life, homes with these features accommodate multiple generations to live together in one home.

Because a home with universal design features allows for independence by having at least one exterior door with no steps, residents who use wheelchairs are not restricted to staying in their homes. They can also invite guests who use wheelchairs to visit in their homes. This freedom of entering and leaving a home reduces social isolation. If more homes were built with universal design features, people of all disabilities and ages would be able to visit their friends, neighbors, and family. They would in turn feel good that their homes were accessible to all people.

Mark and I were consumed with finding information about universal and accessible design. Accessible design describes specific features that are needed to accommodate a person's disability. Examples of accessible design features are grab bars by the toilet and large toe kicks at the base of cabinets.

We researched universal and accessible design by going to the library and brought home giant stacks of books with house plans, floor plans, check lists, photos, and architectural styles. We dedicated ourselves to reading newsletters and articles in magazines and on the Internet.

We cut photos out of magazines, collected product brochures at trade shows and manufacturer's showrooms and filed them for later use. We went to our local independent living center and met with the director, Beverly Rackett. She allowed us access to her library and file folders and graciously made copies of any pages in these documents.

As we met people who used wheelchairs, we asked them about the

Universal Design Toolkit

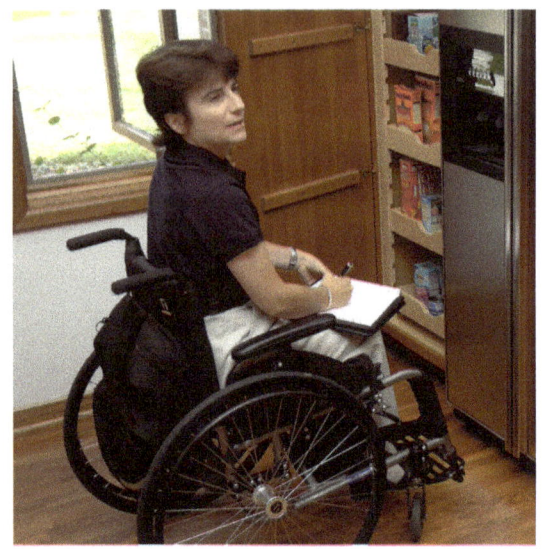

features in their homes that made life easier. We were invited into many homes and allowed to take photos. We interviewed the family members who lived there and asked what features worked and what changes they would make to their homes. We took notes and photos of the homes we toured and saved them in file folders and on our computers. Some of the homes were newly built while others were remodeled homes built for accessibility. I also traveled to other states, when it coordinated with my speaking engagements, to tour universal design homes and interviewed the builder and/or homeowners.

After months of searching for homes and reviewing existing floor plans from builders, we found nothing that would work for us so we began to sketch out our own floor plan.

The 10 Year Project Begins: Selecting a House Location, Architect, and Builder

The home building process began with choosing a location. We wanted to continue living in Columbus, Ohio, so we began to drive around looking for our ideal location. We found a new subdivision where two builders had several home sites available. However, we became discouraged because each builder had only one ranch-style floor plan to offer.

Our previous home was 2,300 square feet combined on the first and second floors. We wanted the new home to be larger than our current home to accommodate wider hallways, and larger bathrooms, kitchen, master closet, laundry, two bedrooms, and two home offices. We also

 Universal Design Toolkit

wanted to have the option to have other family members live with us in the future.

Based on referrals, we chose our builder and put a deposit on a home site. Our builder told us we could modify his existing floor plan by erasing all interior walls and redrawing a new floor plan within the original house footprint. As Mark and I attempted to modify the plan, we quickly became overwhelmed and searched for an architect.

Three architects were interviewed. Architect Patrick Manley, RA, AIAA,

came to our home with his assistant and feng shui design consultant, Cathy Van Volkenburg. Mark and I knew little about feng shui, a Chinese philosophy that is geared at bringing harmony into an environment.

Manley brought us his reference list and described previous projects where he worked on the Americans with Disabilities Act compliant housing projects, as well as residential universal design. We hired Manley in September 2004.

 Universal Design Toolkit

Approaching the Home Design Process

In the next few months, we held several meetings with Manley and Van Volkenburg in which we tried to "shoe horn" our room and space needs into the builder's existing house footprint. We realized we were spinning our wheels, and this approach to designing our new home was not working. The only logical solution would be to create a unique floor plan from scratch.

As Manley presented blueprints to us, we monitored the square footage to keep the costs down. The house was designed from the inside out. That is, first we positioned the rooms in relation to each other. Then we sized each room based on our furniture placement and pathways of travel for my wheelchair. We considered "point of use" when locating appliances in the rooms and rooms within the house. Finally, the exterior shell of the home was detailed.

The new ranch-style home was to have 3,500 square feet of space on the main floor, consisting of: two bedrooms, two home offices, 2-1/2 bathrooms, kitchen, great room, laundry/wardrobe, and library in the hallway. There would be an elevator to access the lower level. This level would include an additional bedroom/office and bathroom, and storage space. We were concerned about the added cost of this larger home.

Then, something amazing happened as we entered the discovery phase of planning and building our home. People started to give us new ideas and their support to fund the construction.

In the fall of 2004, I met a National Association of Home Builders representative at the Greater Columbus Convention Center. I told her I was planning to build a new universal design home and that I was a professional speaker. She gave me two complimentary tickets to attend the upcoming International Builders Show (IBS) in Orlando, FL. She was interested in having me attend this show so that I could learn more about universal design and perhaps speak at a future IBS.

Universal Design Toolkit

In January 2005, Mark and I went to the IBS show. We attended the trade show and seminars. We met with product manufacturers, architects, interior designers, and universal design experts. We brought our home floor plans with us and asked architects and universal design experts to review them and offer suggestions for improvements.

One of the seminar speakers was kitchen and bath designer and internationally renowned universal design specialist and author, Mary Jo Peterson, CKD, CBD, CAPS. I attended her presentation and met with her during lunch to show her our floor plans. We quickly saw her universal design expertise. I asked her to be our interior designer and she agreed. We hired her to work with Manley, guiding our design decisions in the kitchen, bathrooms, and wardrobe.

She also helped in selecting appliances, cabinets and plumbing fixtures.

While meeting with product manufacturers at IBS, one of the representatives asked if Mark and I planned to install a whole house natural gas generator in our new home. We told him that would be a great idea to have power restored during an electrical outage. He said he would arrange to get us one. He gave us brochures about gas generators, his business card and told us he would be in contact.

THE STORY

As we left his booth Mark and I asked each other if this man had just offered to GIVE us a generator! We both thought that this was his intent and were delighted with this generous offer. I was eager to follow up with this man when I returned to Columbus.

Going from a Private Residence to a Public Demonstration Home

Mark and I intended that the home we were building would be our private residence. We thought about inviting a few people to see it when it was completed so others could learn from it. A major turning point in the project occurred during a meeting in Orlando on January 21, 2005, the weekend after we attended the IBS.

A mastermind group of which Mark and I belonged gave us the idea to build a national demonstration home. The ten of us in this mastermind group were professional speakers, trainers, writers and consultants, all with different areas of expertise. This was our first face to face meeting with this group. Prior to this date, we had only been on group phone conferences together. They first learned about our interest in building a universal design home on a conference call.

Mark and I introduced ourselves and told them about our experiences a few days earlier at the IBS and the conversation with the representative

Mastermind Group, from left to right: Jeff Warren, Peter Land, Rick Dudnick, Pam Lontos, Dawn Josephson, Gerry Murak, Rosemarie, David Josephson, Stan Craig

from the gas generator company. This ignited the mastermind members' conversations. The group suggested that our home not only be universal design but also be sustainable and green, utilize the latest technology, and be open to the public as well as the building and design industries. They recommended we find corporate contributors, and that I speak internationally about universal design and green building practices.

This was one BIG idea — a national demonstration home that was supported by corporate sponsors! Mark and I took lots of notes and tried to comprehend what this group was suggesting. I particularly had trouble understanding due to the large scope of the project.

I shared a story with the group that had occurred on July 16, 2004. I was delivering a motivational keynote speech near St. Charles, IL for Aquascape, a leading water garden product distributor. After my presentation, the 200 distributors in the audience gave me a standing ovation! The CEO, Greg Wittstock came to the stage and when the applause was over he announced to the audience that he wanted to give me and Mark a pond for our home someday. This was the first contribution to our home that sparked the idea that I might be able to speak for other corporations in exchange for products.

The mastermind group was super excited and encouraging around the conference room table that day as they continued to build on each other's ideas for our new home. They pledged to continue to give us ideas and help when needed. They sent us back to Columbus with lots on our minds to think about. How could we ever pull this off? Where do we begin?

Securing Corporate Contributors and Partners

Mark and I returned home from that meeting, slowly began to absorb the suggestions of the mastermind group, and moved into action. We began contacting international, national and local corporate contributors.

Universal Design Toolkit

In September 2005, Bill Gerhardt, president/founder and landscape architect of GreenScapes Landscape Company agreed to contribute his design services for the landscape. We met to discuss the general design and needs for accessibility.

In October 2005, we hired S. Robert August of Denver, Colorado as our marketing consultant. He was our biggest cheerleader throughout the construction project and beyond, giving us momentum, direction, encouragement and hope. He led the efforts to obtain the contributors of products and services for the home.

S. Robert August

He created the Menu of Sponsorship Opportunities that served us well in our discussions with potential contributors. August introduced us to decision makers in the marketing and sales departments of major corporations, thus opening the door to dialogue. He told us that we needed to be in constant communication with each of our contributors and that we needed to send out an electronic monthly newsletter to let them know the progress of the design and construction, updates, and information about public relations activities that we had initiated.

August named our home the Universal Design Living Laboratory (UDLL). He has been integral in making our dream become a reality through his team's creative and pragmatic talents.

Through August's training, Mark and I became proficient in calling product manufacturers and sales representatives to ask them to contribute products and services for the Universal Design Living

Laboratory. We continued calling and coordinating the delivery of products from 2005 - 2014 through the entire construction process.

Going beyond our wildest dream, a total of 217 contributors generously supported us by either contributing their products and services, providing discounts on their products and services, and/or installing their products. We could not have built this home without them. These contributors were a significant factor in making this national demonstration home and garden a reality. Contributors are listed at http://www.udll.com

Each of the contributors made a significant investment in the project. They believed in Mark and me and knew the time had come to build a home to showcase their universal design and green building products. They also understood that they were not just contributing to Mark and my home, but to a bigger purpose. This home could inspire others including the home design and building industry. This home could give hope to people who are struggling in their current homes.

This tribe of loyal people not only gave us their products and services, they also gave us design ideas and other product and service suggestions. They sent us emails of encouragement. They introduced us to other contributors who supplied products and services. They visited the UDLL during the construction process and offered guidance. They wrote testimonial letters. They directed the media to us on a national level so we could get featured articles in major magazines, in company and association newsletters, and on blogs. They looked for speaking opportunities for Mark and me and oftentimes sponsored me to speak at national universal design conferences. They became our friends.

As the home design process continued, I called upon one of my best friends, Anna Lyon, who is an interior designer. She was the interior designer on my three previous homes. We hired her to review the floor plans and elevations, and make suggestions for improvements. She also assisted us by drawing furniture to scale on the floor plan. She went with us to local home shows for several consecutive years helping us select colors and get design ideas.

Universal Design Toolkit

In the final design phase, she helped select colors and finishes for the cabinets and walls, flooring, countertops, tile, plumbing and lighting fixtures. She went with Mark and me in June 2007 to the Kohler national showroom in Wisconsin to select our plumbing fixtures. In October 2009 Lyon went with us to the KraftMaid Cabinetry showroom in Middlefield, Ohio to help design and select our cabinets. She made several trips with us to tile, flooring, and lighting fixture showrooms.

Mark and I went to local builder home shows for several consecutive years to see their newest model homes. We also went to local home and garden shows annually during the design and construction process.

Anna Lyon with Rosemarie

In January 2006, Mark and I went to Orlando again and attended the IBS, sponsored by the National Association of Home Builders. I was a speaker at this conference with Mary Jo Peterson, and builders Derek Layer and Dottie Harper. I talked about the Universal Design Living Laboratory universal design features and the need for universal design. Our presentation "Successful Universal Design: Eliminate the Fear Factor" was delivered to a standing room only crowd of builders.

Mark and I spent several days on the massive trade show exhibit floor to look at products and talk with sales representatives about potential sponsorship opportunities. August introduced us to people he knew and opened the conversations for us. We attended seminars and met with architects who reviewed our house plans and offered suggestions

Universal Design Toolkit

for improvement. Industry experts in the field of universal design networked around us and freely offered their help and advice during this design phase.

At a social function at IBS, I became re-acquainted with lighting design expert Patricia Rizzo, Adjunct Assistant Professor from the Lighting Research Center at the Rensselaer Polytechnic Institute in Troy, NY. She offered to have her seven graduate students create an interior lighting design of our home as a project. I made final plans to take a flight to Troy, NY in mid-January 2006 to deliver a presentation and meet with her and the seven graduate students to begin the interior lighting design project.

As result of Rizzo and me meeting, we decided to put together a team presentation on universal design lighting considerations. We delivered "A Home You Can Grow Old In" with architect Robert Williams for the National Association of Home Builders at the 50+ Housing Symposium in Phoenix, on April 25, 2006.

Patricia Rizzo (right) and graduate students from Rensselaer Polytechnic Institute

Project Stalls and New Directions

In February 2006, our builder, Mark and I went to the sub-division where the lot that we had chosen in 2004 was located. We met with the homeowner's association board of directors to discuss the UDLL project. Unfortunately they asked us not to build in their neighborhood because they didn't want the traffic and tour visitors. Mark and I were dumbfounded! We released the lot back to the builder. Our project was delayed for several more months.

We immediately set out to find a new home site that was not in a sub-division. In April 2006, Mark spotted a 1.5 acre lot for sale by owner. From April until the deal was closed in December 2006, we worked with the owner to purchase her land.

This new larger lot in a rural setting inspired us to meet with Manley to re-design the house. Since he no longer was bound by any architectural guidelines from a homeowner's association, he could design our home to be more creative. Robert August suggested a re-design of the exterior to enhance its curb appeal. Inspired by the famed architect Frank Lloyd Wright, Manley created a new Prairie style architecture look with a clerestory roofline and a prominent portico at the front entrance.

Our biggest contributor, Marvin Windows and Doors, announced their contribution of all the windows and patio doors, and the installation of these windows and doors at no cost, in July of 2006. Dale Schmitz, Marketing Manager, wrote this testimonial:

> *Universal Design is no longer a concept to be considered only by the physically challenged or those looking to age in place, but is a full-fledged planning methodology that is gaining momentum with building professionals and architects. The UDLL will be a living and evolving showcase for those who seek the best practices in human centered design and accessibility solutions. Rosemarie Rossetti and her husband, Mark Leder, shared the mission for the UDLL with me earlier this year. During that conversation I*

was able to learn about all of the great promotional activities they have planned and more importantly, about their passion and commitment to make the UDLL a cutting-edge resource that will serve the advancement of universal design well into the future."

In August 2007, we learned that our builder had gone out of business. This came as a major blow and further delayed construction. After many builder interviews in the summer of 2007, Mark and I decided to build the home as the general contractors, and hired Bob White and Chris Vandenoever as our construction consultants.

In February 2008, Mark and I met with Ardra Zinkon, lighting designer with Tec Inc. Engineering & Design. Because of the home's exterior architectural makeover and substantial changes to the interior space, Zinkon agreed to re-design the lighting.

Many people became our allies and champions. They gave us momentum. Our representative from the Ohio House of Representatives, Marion Harris, wrote this testimonial letter on May 6, 2009:

> "On behalf of the Ohio House of Representatives, I congratulate you on your efforts to introduce the Universal Design Living Laboratory, to be built in Jefferson Township, to central Ohio. Your interest in building this demonstration home to help educate private, institutional and public sectors about the importance of energy and water conservation, universal design features, and state-of-the-art products and services is a unique educational contribution."

 Universal Design Toolkit

Home Construction Begins

It took Mark and me several years to acquire a construction loan due to the building and loan recession. During this delay of trying to get a loan, more contributors were acquired. This helped us by having more signed agreements proving to the bank that major corporations were contributing products and services for the construction. We had to reduce our construction costs through contributions of products and services in order to have a construction budget within our financial means.

In August 2009, Jim Long, President of the Middlefield Banking Company (formerly known as Emerald Bank), approved our loan. He was the only banker who understood what we were doing, trusted the corporations who had pledged their contributions, and believed Mark and I could be successful building our home.

Jim Long (left) with Rosemarie and Mark

The groundbreaking ceremony was on September 23, 2009. We were overwhelmed when we saw about 100 people in attendance at the home site including our banker, the local media, contributors, neighbors, family, friends, and elected representatives from the U.S., State, County, and Township. We received six proclamations and resolutions from government entities praising the work that Mark and I were doing by building the Universal Design Living Laboratory. All of the people at the groundbreaking wanted to be a part of this momentous occasion and cheered us on!

**Universal Design Toolkit**

Groundbreaking ceremony, from left to right: Rudy Leder, Richard Rossetti, Rose Rossetti, Bob White, Rosemarie, Mark, Pat Manley and Chris Vandenoever

As the general contractors, Mark and I worked doggedly for the next 32 months on the design and construction. We hired and supervised the subcontractors, recruited and supervised volunteers, acquired contributors, created construction drawing details, and paid all the bills. Our two construction consultants and our architect were called in from time to time to evaluate the work, offer guidance and suggest changes.

Mark was on site all the time. He is very resourceful and learned quickly how to do things. He had some experience in construction growing up with his father. To save us money he did portions of the work himself including some plumbing, electrical, carpentry, and insulating. He took photos daily and videotaped the installation process on several occasions.

Scott Cunningham Photography

THE STORY

45

During the entire construction process, there was a camera mounted on a tall pole in the front corner of the property that took a photo of the construction site every 30 seconds. Those photos were shown live on our website.

We had thousands of decisions to make regarding the final design and product selection. Mark created hundreds of detailed construction drawings on his computer to enable the installers to assemble all the parts that made up our home.

Mark also led the documentation and application process for three universal design certification programs: Livable Design, ZeroStep, and Life-Flex Home. In addition he did all of the documentation and application process for the two national green building programs: LEED for Homes by the U.S. Green Building Council and the National Green Building Standard program.

There were many delays during construction due to:

- a need to have more corporations contribute products and services
- the project going over budget
- our limited personal finances
- bad weather
- difficulty finding sub-contractors and volunteers
- sub-contractors not being on the job
- problems with the design and installation

Mark and I had never built a house before and had much to learn. We made mistakes. Solutions had to be found quickly to resolve them.

There were many sleepless nights and worrisome days. Mark and I did our best to be optimistic, but the reality was right in front of us every

day as we went to the construction site to face the magnitude of the project and the daunting task at hand.

This was most evident to Mark one morning in October 2009 when he went to the construction site and saw the excavator in operation. The operator had begun digging the home foundation. Mark saw the deep hole, the size of two rooms of our home. When he came home, Mark told me, "I had a lump in my throat and a knot in my stomach. I sighed with a feeling of fear and trepidation. There's no turning back now."

What got us through the hard times was our firm belief that our home was going to help a lot of people. Our home would give individuals and families hope knowing that there are solutions to the housing problems

Universal Design Toolkit

THE STORY

48

Universal Design Toolkit

they faced due to a lack of accessible features. The project was more than just building a home for Mark and me. The project was bigger and the impact it was having on the design and construction industry could be significant. Our home was special not only in the design, but in what it stood for as a model.

We were reassured with every new contributor or volunteer that came to our aid. They made connections for us to other people who would join the project in some way. One connection led to many more. This community of enthusiastic supporters was massive and we knew that we couldn't fail because they were right there helping us to succeed.

We often said to each other, "Failure is not an option." When our plan A didn't work we looked for a plan B. The fear of regret was stronger than the fear of failure. If we didn't finish what we set out to do we would regret it the rest of our lives. We had to pursue in spite of any obstacles that blocked us.

We continued to acquire more contributors and moved forward with the construction. Our success in acquiring contributors gave us more energy and boosted the project's momentum each day.

Early in 2010, Whirlpool agreed to ship ten major appliances that they were contributing. The Manager of Business Development, Terri Connett knew that our home was not at that point in the construction to install these appliances. She had trust in us that they would be installed. My cousin, Frank Mascari, agreed to store these appliances in his warehouse until January 2012 when they were installed in our home.

On March 5, 2010 Mark and I went to Classic Metal Roofing Systems to observe the manufacturing process of the recycled aluminum roof they had contributed. I had delivered a motivational presentation to their dealers the night before. Todd E. Miller, President, surprised us in a meeting by introducing us to a solar panel corporate partner who contributed a roof solar panel that would be integrated into our roof.

On October 8, 2010, six years after my speech at Aquascape, the promise made to me by CEO Greg Wittstock to build a water feature in our yard was fulfilled. The 40 person installation team was made up of Aquascape key corporate staff, employees of distributors from a four state area, and horticulture students from Hocking College. The project was designed as a hands-on teaching and training day. The day began with a large mound of compacted soil in the landscape. By days end, the result was a beautiful four tiered waterfall and rainwater harvesting system.

Greg Wittstock (standing on bridge, second from left)

Also in October 2010, we sold our previous home we had built in 1995 and moved to a small minimally-accessible apartment where Mark and I lived for the remaining 19 months of construction.

Mark and I continued our pursuit of contributors. In May 2011 we travelled to Sugar Creek, Ohio and visited with the ProVia company representatives to design the front door and watch the manufacturing process. The sales staff was not familiar with universal design. We explained that the front door needed a center glass section with peepholes positioned at various eyelevel heights so either Mark or I could see who was on the front porch.

Universal Design Toolkit

During the design and construction process, I was writing articles for numerous national magazines. From March 2006 – June 2011, I wrote a monthly "Accessible Home" column in Action magazine, a publication of the United Spinal Association. I also spoke nationally delivering presentations to the building and design industry about our home.

When all the inspections were approved and we obtained an occupancy permit we made plans to move into our dream home. The landscape had not been installed and the basement was not finished.

On May 18, 2012, the moving vans pulled up our driveway and Mark and I moved into our new home. That was one memorable homecoming!

For the next two years, work continued to obtain more contributors in order to install the landscape. This included the retaining walls, patio pavers, plants, and grass seed. Landscape horticulturist and owner of the Ivy Tree, Tom Lehner, was a co-instructor with me when I taught horticulture during the 1970's at the Delaware Area Career Center. He helped with: acquiring sponsors; the design of the landscape; selecting plants; planting plants; and installing the retaining walls and pavers.

Tom Lehner (green jacket, kneeling)

Universal Design Toolkit

Tracy DiSabato-Aust, landscape horticulturist, and garden writer, designed the front landscape beds.

Volunteers including students, neighbors, friends and corporate partners participated in the installation of nearly all the landscape plant materials, pavers and walls.

The final area to be completed was the basement, having a full bathroom, bedroom, exercise room, and group meeting room. It was Mark and my intention to have the basement become a learning/gathering/training space to share our experience building the Universal Design Living Laboratory. It would also provide a place for visitors to stay and experience the home.

Additional product manufacturers were secured for the basement. This included drywall, insulation, ceiling tiles, floor tiles, ceiling lights, paint, and meeting room furniture. Volunteers did some of the work finishing the basement including painting, installing ceiling tiles, and putting in wall insulation.

With the landscape and basement projects completed, the time had come to plan for the public tours. Additional contributors and volunteers were secured to support these tours. Nationwide Insurance was the leading sponsor for the 30 days of public tours from October 25

through November 23, 2014. They supplied 50 MP3 audio players and paid to have a professional female voice talent record the script that Mark and I wrote for the narrated tours.

There were 546 people who toured our home, including 60 volunteers. Several dozen artists loaned their artwork to be displayed in the home. Net proceeds from the tour benefitted my spinal cord injury research project at The Ohio State University Wexner Medical Center.

The National Demonstration Home and Garden

The years of research into the area of universal design transformed Mark and me. The process led to a belief that we could share our research, knowledge, and our home to make a significant and positive difference in the lives of others to increase their quality of life. We were passionate about finding a way to share what we had learned with others. We wanted to show others that homes could be designed to accommodate them for the rest of their lives. We wanted to give others, who were struggling with their current home environment, hope that there are solutions to make their lives easier. This desire to help others was our driving force that kept us going through the hardships and stalls along the way.

Our home is the national demonstration home and garden in Columbus, Ohio. It is the top-rated universal design home in North America earning three national certifications:

- Livable Design,
- ZeroStep, and
- Life-Flex Home.

It was also built with green building principles and has been certified:

- Silver level in the LEED for Homes program by the U.S. Green Building Council.

 Universal Design Toolkit

- Gold level from the National Green Building Standard program (National Association of Home Builders).

It was also recognized a Certified Wildlife Habitat by the National Wildlife Federation.

Living in our home is a privilege. We are well aware of how the universal design features provide accessibility, independence,

safety, convenience, and peace of mind. We are so grateful for the contributions of time, money, products and labor from thousands of contributors, partners, and volunteers. We are also grateful to our parents for their financial and emotional support and continued love.

What Helped Prepare Me to Take On the UDLL Project?

In reflection, I think about my past experiences, education and my life before my disability. I wondered what prepared me to take on this project.

My college education undergraduate majors were in agricultural education and horticulture. My Masters and Ph.D. degrees were in agricultural education. I taught classes in teaching methods, public speaking, and marketing at The Ohio State University in the Department of Agricultural Education for eleven years. I taught horticulture at a vocational high school for three years and wrote the book, The Healthy Indoor Plant. I was a vice president of sales and marketing at an interior landscaping firm for eight years.

The knowledge I learned from these experiences and my education served me well. That knowledge and experience were the foundation that helped me organize and execute the UDLL project.

With my background as an expert speaker and teacher as well as my experience as a writer, I was able to communicate with others. I used my sales and marketing experience and applied it to a new situation. I knew how to speak with a potential contributor and discuss the benefit of being our partner.

Tenacity was a trait that others recognized in me as a child. Once I got an idea to do something, I did everything in my power to learn how to get it done and focus on completing my goal.

This trait was especially important right after my injury. I wanted to recover. I wrote the book, *Take Back Your Life!* to share the life lessons I learned the first two years of my recovery. These lessons helped me during the design and construction of our home.

The most influential factor in my life that helped me throughout the UDLL project was my loving husband Mark Leder. I married him three years before I was injured. He was and is my best friend. We worked as a team in constant communication. We supported each other through all the trials and tribulations. We celebrated our achievements together. We worked hard and never lost sight of why we were building our new home — to make a positive difference in the lives of other through better home design.

A Desire to Share What We've Learned

During our new home design and construction journey from 2004 – 2014, we dedicated ourselves to this project. Mark and I have learned and discovered much in our journey.

I came back to our home in 1998 after my injury. For the next 12 years, Mark I were able to study my day-to-day movement and how I tried to function in the home. We took lots of photos and notes in that home to help us in the design of our new home.

The cramped apartment that we temporarily moved to in October 2010 because of our previous home's sale, further intensified my frustration. I came to fully understand how difficult it was to find an apartment (or any housing for that matter) that could even minimally meet my needs.

We have shared what we learned by showing our home to thousands of other people by allowing them to take a tour. We also shared the stage as we spoke and presented photos of the home construction and of each of the features in our completed home. We have consulted with consumer, builders, remodelers, architects, Realtors, and developers to help them with their projects. I have written many articles and been interviewed by many journalists for their articles. I have created videos and webinars to showcase the features and explain the benefits of universal design, accessible design, and green building. We continue our outreach and share our expertise so others can benefit.

We are sharing some of the information that we assembled, compiled and utilized during the design and building of our socially sustainable home through this Universal Design Toolkit. Mark and I know what works and what doesn't. We put our hearts into creating this book so that others could benefit through our combined knowledge and years of experience.

We ask you to read the Universal Design Toolkit and apply what you learned to your projects. Incorporate universal design products and features in future homes. Whether it is your own home or a client's home, there are many ideas, shortcuts, resources, suggestions, and guidance to help you create a home that makes life easier.

When you need our help along the way, we are only a phone call or email away. We are YOUR universal design resource! Feel free to contact us to consult with you or deliver a presentation.

The Universal Design Living Laboratory will act as a resource to learn from – today and tomorrow. See the listing of contributors, take a virtual tour, watch videos, read articles, see resources and learn more at: http://www.udll.com

INTRODUCTION

Thank you for purchasing the Universal Design Toolkit! I hope that you find high value in your toolkit and that it is used often and serves you well.

As the creator of this collection of information and resources, I hope that this Universal Design Toolkit makes it easier for you to complete your current and future home design projects.

What is universal design?

To get started, you need to know what universal design is. Universal design is a framework for the design of living and working spaces and products, benefiting the widest possible range of people in the widest range of situations without special or separate design.

Universal design is human-centered design, accommodating people of all sizes, ages, and abilities. A home designed with universal design principles certainly makes life easier, not only for those with mobility limitations, but also for those who are young, old, short or tall.

The goal of universal design is to give the user more independence, accessibility, safety, convenience and peace of mind.

Universal design homes are for everyone!

- A person with a mobility limitation, caused by an injury or disease, either short term or long term, will have an easier time getting in and out of a home. They will also find universal design homes have more space to function in, especially in the kitchen and bathrooms.

- Multiple generations of families will find homes with universal design features to be a benefit. The home will be immediately useable as family members grow and change.

- Social isolation is prevented as friends and family with physical challenges can easily visit, enter and use a home having universal design features.

What is the Universal Design Toolkit and the Universal Design Living Laboratory?

The Universal Design Toolkit is the first of its kind containing a wealth of information. This toolkit is not theoretical but rather a practical collection of information and resources. It is a distillation of knowledge and experience realized from ten years of research, site visits, consults with experts, and numerous design evaluations. The Universal Design Living Laboratory, the home my husband Mark Leder and I live in, is the result of our efforts.

Scott Cunningham Photography

You can learn about the Universal Design Living Laboratory at our website http://www.udll.com **Our website is a companion to this Universal Design Toolkit.**

- Take a virtual tour to see the universal design features and products

- Go on a video tour led by Mark Leder to see the universal design features and products

 Universal Design Toolkit

- See the contributors who provided products and services along with links to their websites

- See the floor plan

- Watch videos about the Universal Design Living Laboratory

- Watch Rosemarie Rossetti's webinar replays

- Read articles written in national publications about the Universal Design Living Laboratory

- Read Rosemarie Rossetti's articles about accessible housing and universal design

- See the many additional resource links and be instantly connected to more information

Why was the Universal Design Toolkit written?

This mastery toolkit was designed by Mark and me with these purposes in mind.

- To share what we have learned so that others could incorporate universal design features into their living environments.

- To make life easier for people by helping them design homes that provide more independence, accessibility, safety, convenience and peace of mind so the homes are livable for a lifetime.

- To enhance others quality of life by improving the conditions of their home environments.

We saw the surging trend of the aging population and a shortage of housing to accommodate both this population, as well as people with disabilities. People should be able to stay in their homes for as long as possible before moving to assisted living or nursing facilities.

Universal Design Toolkit

Jack Johnston / J Stroke Creative

As you can see, I use a wheelchair for mobility. This is a result of an accident on June 13, 1998. While riding my bicycle, suddenly I was crushed by a 3-1/2 ton tree and sustained a spinal cord injury leaving me paralyzed from the waist down. The home that I was living in at the time intensified my disability was a source of continued frustration. Mark and I knew that we had to sell that home and find more suitable wheelchair accessible housing. Our solution was to build a new home that would accommodate both of us for the rest of our lives.

Who is the Universal Design Toolkit for?

- **Consumers** including those who are:

    - considering to continue to live in (and thus remodel) their existing home

    - wanting to build a new home

    - wanting to "rightsize" and move to a home/condo/apartment that will better meet their current and long term needs

    - faced with housing decisions and potential modifications because of a family member's advanced age, accident, medical emergency or special needs child

- **Professionals who market and sell to the housing industry**, such as:

    - housing developers who want to attract the 50+ market and forward thinking individuals and families to their developments

 Universal Design Toolkit

- architects, planners, interior designers, and landscape designers who desire to create additional value added knowledge and services to better address their client's needs

- builders and remodelers who want to include universal design features into their projects

- Realtors to better guide their clients to housing more appropriate for their needs, and to better describe the attributes in homes they are listing for sale

■ **Professionals who provide services to consumers**, including:

- occupational therapists who are working with their clients to make home modifications to support independence in day to day living

- caregivers who are working with their clients to help make their lives easier

■ **Educators** who want to inspire their students to gain awareness, embrace compassion, and develop actionable vision and goals for meeting the needs of a rapidly expanding underserved population.

What is in the Universal Design Toolkit and how can it be used?

The Table of Contents provides an overview. There is no particular order by which you should open a chapter, document or link. Let your curiosity guide you. **You can navigate quickly from chapter to chapter by clicking on the name of the chapter in the Table of Contents.**

Chapter 1 will introduce you to the benefits of universal design. The features allow for more independence, accessibility, safety, convenience and peace of mind.

 Universal Design Toolkit

Included in this chapter is a collection of words and phrases to help you communicate these concepts to others. To help those professionals wanting to attract new business, these same words and phrases (along with benefit statements about universal design) can help make your marketing copywriting efforts more compelling and memorable.

In Chapter 2, you will discover the seven universal design principles that guide the design process.

In Chapter 3, I will dispel the ten myths I discovered about universal design.

There are an abundance of terms tossed around in the field of universal design. Chapter 4 contains a glossary to help define, differentiate and clarify these terms.

Chapter 5 is a ready reference of the most important space dimensions when designing homes for people who use wheelchairs and walkers for mobility.

For those professionals who are working with clients, see the Chapter 6 questionnaire so that you can find out what their current and future housing needs are as you work with them during the design process.

Oftentimes, people with limited incomes, people with disabilities, and veterans need funding for the modification of their current home or the construction of a new home. Sources of funding and low interest loan programs have been identified and are included in Chapter 7.

For consumers, Chapter 8 can be your starting point to help you find a builder, remodeler, architect, home designer, Realtor, lighting designer, interior designer, landscape designer, and occupational therapist who is knowledgeable about universal design. See the many professional organizations and associations and the universal design certification programs and courses available to their members.

Universal Design Toolkit

Once you've created a shortlist of potential designers, builders and/or remodelers to hire, I have provided a questionnaire in Chapter 9 that you as a consumer can use during the interview process to help you decide who to hire.

Sometimes, it makes more sense to follow the experiences of others when planning your project. You can use the Chapter 10 resources to view house plans and floor plans as a thought starter. Or jump start your project with house plans and floor plans that are ready to go.

Chapter 11 lays out the estimated construction and product costs of including selected universal design features and products.

Chapter 12 is the checklist of the universal design features, room by room, at the Universal Design Living Laboratory.

I've compiled a vast collection of checklists from around the world in Chapter 13. You'd be hard pressed with these checklists to miss a single feature when you're designing a home with universal design, safety, and convenience in mind. Also referenced are the three universal design certification programs that were followed when building the Universal Design Living Laboratory. Each of these programs has its own checklist of universal design features.

For real estate professionals, developers, and builders, Chapter 14 details the findings from recent research noting that home buyer's needs for accessible housing are unmet. This will help professionals better understand their role linking buyers to the right home.

To help you understand the concept of visitability, see the Chapter 15 summary of recent research showing the perceived value of visitable housing. Visitability refers to the basic features in a home that would allow people who use wheelchairs or walkers the ability to enter the home for a visit.

Chapter 16 contains a multitude of resources and includes a comprehensive collection of books and printed materials on the subject of universal design.

 Universal Design Toolkit

How can I contact Rosemarie Rossetti, Ph.D. and learn more about her speaking and consulting services?

If ever you have a question or need additional information, don't hesitate to contact Rosemarie. Rosemarie@udll.com Mark and Rosemarie are available to consult with you, work with you on a home plan or development project. They travel the country delivering presentations and encourage you to consider them for upcoming programs. To learn more about Rosemarie, visit her speaking business website at http://www.RosemarieSpeaks.com

John Evans Photography

1 BENEFITS OF HAVING UNIVERSAL DESIGN FEATURES IN HOMES

Long Term Cost Savings

- Families can save money in the long term when universal design features are a part of the original construction. When universal design features are included, this greatly reduces the likelihood that the home will need to be remodeled should a family member face an injury or illness. The home will be accessible and provide more independence.

- With the convenience and accessibility of universal design features, it is less likely for a family member to have to move to an assisted living facility. There is a choice available to stay at home and have care provided in the home. Home care provided in a home on an as needed basis is significantly more cost effective than moving to an assisted living facility. There is direct control over the quality and quantity of care that can be provided by having caregivers come to the home.

Multigenerational

A home with universal design features can be occupied by many generations of families, since people of all ages are considered when designing these homes.

Rosemarie's family

 Universal Design Toolkit

Increased Home Value

- Faster home sales.

- Improved marketability when the home is for sale. Increased home retail value. Higher resale value.

- Aesthetically beautiful.

- For rental units, the accessible apartments will likely be the first to be rented.

- Greater longevity of the home's value, not just to the people who live there now, but to those who will live there in the future.

Better Quality of Life

Universal design features support living in your home for a lifetime. These features allow the residents to age comfortably in their homes.

Retaining Independence

Daily living skills like transferring in and out of bed, toileting, showering, and cooking are easier to accomplish without barriers when universal design features are included. Barriers in the home are eliminated when features such as step-free entrances, grab bars, curbless showers, 36" wide doors, 30" high counters, and reachable cabinets are included.

Universal Design Toolkit

Enhanced Peace of Mind

There are fewer worries knowing that aging family members are supported by their home environment and life is easier for them in a universal design home. In life there will be unforeseen circumstances and changes from a temporary or permanent disability that impact how we live. The goal is to create homes that are livable for a lifetime, so the occupants are accommodated and confident that they don't have to prematurely move out.

More Safety

There are fewer risks of falls, slips, trips, burns, back strain, and dizzy spells that lead to injuries. Safety features in a universal design home include: curbless shower, enhanced lighting for aging eyes, low glare surfaces and light fixtures, motion sensor lighting, slip resistant tile, grab bars, step-free entrances, and flush door thresholds.

More Convenient and Functional

Less time will be spent and less stress, strain, and frustration will be experienced with universal design features such as: pull out shelves and drawers, reachable storage, countertops at reachable heights, front loading washer and dryer, knee space under sinks and cooktop, handheld shower nozzle, casement windows, and a side hinged oven door.

A side door oven (open), next to a convection microwave.

 Universal Design Toolkit

Feeling of Self-worth and Increased Human Dignity

People feel proud that they are able to better take care of themselves as well as others in the family due to the universal design features that provide independence. People can do the things they want to do independently in the home including working, gardening, activities of daily living, and engaging in hobbies.

Friends and Family Can Visit

A visitable home includes a no step entry, low threshold, and a 36" wide door to allow passage for guests who visit that use wheelchairs, scooters, and walkers. A wheelchair accessible half bath on the first floor with access through a hallway contributes to a positive social environment for all of your guests. You will be more inclusive with your guest list when entertaining in your home.

Homes that are all visitable in a community enable people to be able

to not only visit on social occasions but to also provide and obtain assistance from time to time. A neighborhood where the homes are designed for easy access enables more interaction not only on the front porches but also inside the homes. Isolation can lead to loneliness and depression. Having homes that the occupants can leave independently to visit their neighbors is a great benefit.

Words to Better Communicate the Concept of Universal Design

- Ease of living
- Comfortable
- Sustainable
- Safer
- Easier to access
- More ergonomic
- Adaptable
- Inclusive design
- Flexible housing
- Convenient
- More independence
- Better living design
- Transparent design
- Accessible
- Livable design
- Life span design
- Transgenerational design
- Design for all
- Lifetime homes
- Enabling design

2 THE PRINCIPLES OF UNIVERSAL DESIGN

The authors, a working group of architects, product designers, engineers and environmental design researchers, collaborated to establish the following Principles of Universal Design to guide a wide range of design disciplines including environments, products, and communications. These seven principles may be applied to evaluate existing designs, guide the design process and educate both designers and consumers about the characteristics of more usable products and environments.

Text Copyright © 1997 NC State University, The Center for Universal Design

PRINCIPLE ONE: Equitable Use

The design is useful and marketable to people with diverse abilities.

- Provide the same means of use for all users: identical whenever possible; equivalent when not.

- Avoid segregating or stigmatizing any users.

- Provisions for privacy, security, and safety should be equally available to all users.

- Make the design appealing to all users.

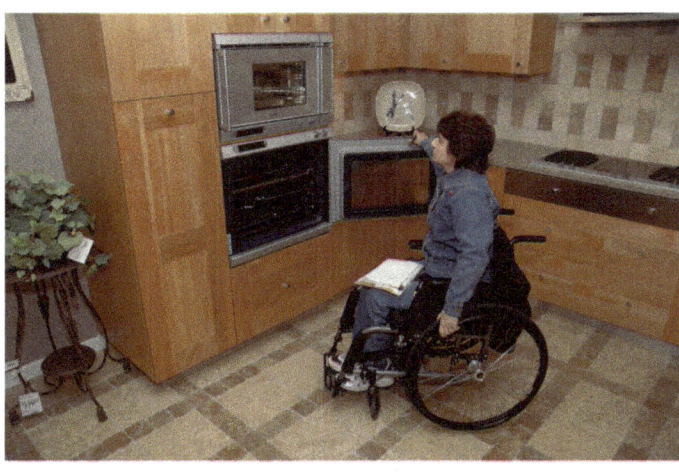
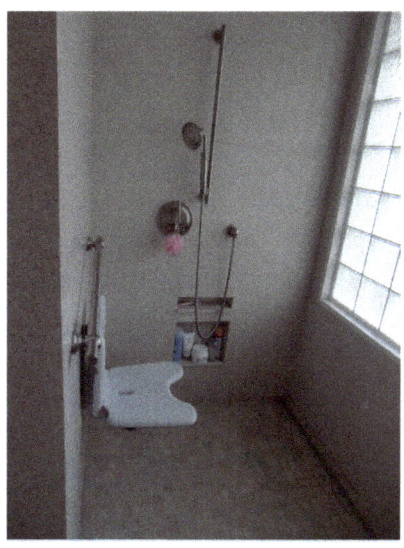

Universal Design Toolkit

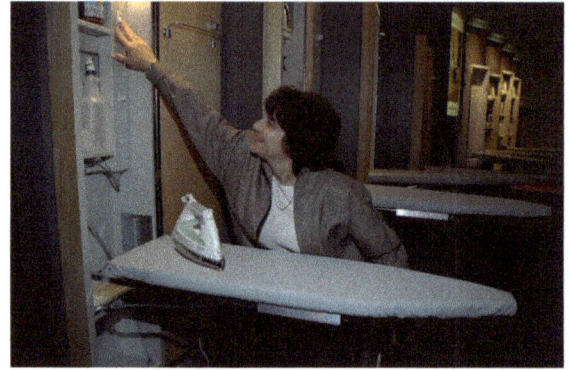

PRINCIPLE TWO: Flexibility in Use
The design accommodates a wide range of individual preferences and abilities.

- Provide choice in methods of use.
- Accommodate right or lefthanded access and use.
- Facilitate the user's accuracy and precision.
- Provide adaptability to the user's pace.

PRINCIPLE THREE: Simple and Intuitive Use
Use of the design is easy to understand, regardless of the user's experience, knowledge, language skills, or current concentration level.

- Eliminate unnecessary complexity.
- Be consistent with user expectations and intuition.
- Accommodate a wide range of literacy and language skills.
- Arrange information consistent with its importance.
- Provide effective prompting and feedback during and after task completion.

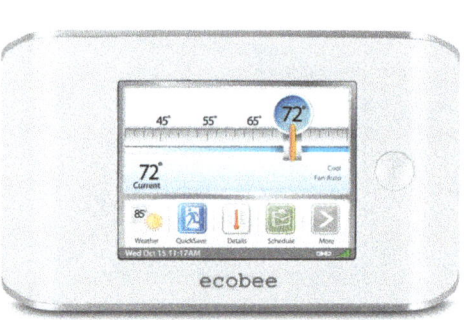

Universal Design Toolkit

PRINCIPLE FOUR: Perceptible Information

The design communicates necessary information effectively to the user, regardless of ambient conditions or the user's sensory abilities.

- Use different modes (pictorial, verbal, tactile) for redundant presentation of essential information.

- Provide adequate contrast between essential information and its surroundings.

- Maximize "legibility" of essential information.

- Differentiate elements in ways that can be described (i.e., make it easy to give instructions or directions).

- Provide compatibility with a variety of techniques or devices used by people with sensory limitations.

 Universal Design Toolkit

PRINCIPLE FIVE: Tolerance for Error

The design minimizes hazards and the adverse consequences of accidental or unintended actions.

- Arrange elements to minimize hazards and errors: most used elements, most accessible; hazardous elements eliminated, isolated, or shielded.
- Provide warnings of hazards and errors.
- Provide fail safe features.
- Discourage unconscious action in tasks that require vigilance.

PRINCIPLE SIX: Low Physical Effort

The design can be used efficiently and comfortably and with a minimum of fatigue.

- Allow user to maintain a neutral body position
- Use reasonable operating forces.
- Minimize repetitive actions.
- Minimize sustained physical effort.

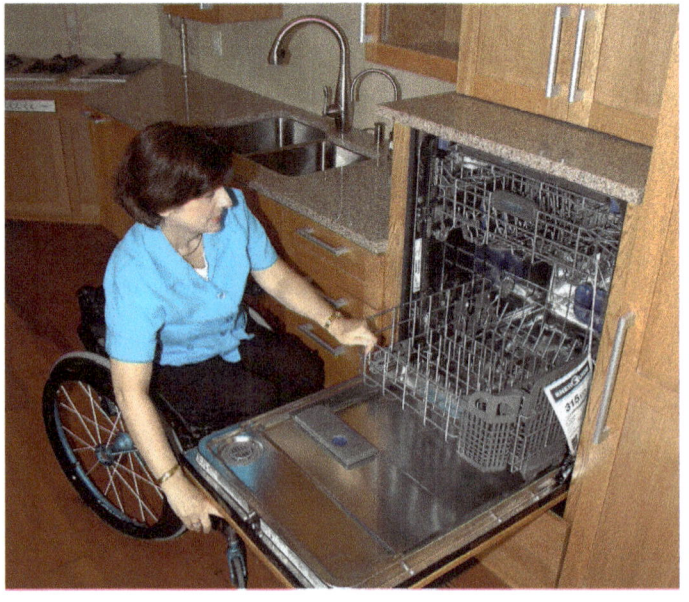

PRINCIPLES

Universal Design Toolkit

PRINCIPLE SEVEN: Size and Space for Approach and Use

Appropriate size and space is provided for approach, reach, manipulation, and use regardless of user's body size, posture, or mobility.

- Provide a clear line of sight to important elements for any seated or standing user.

- Make reach to all components comfortable for any seated or standing user.

- Accommodate variations in hand and grip size.

- Provide adequate space for the use of assistive devices or personal assistance.

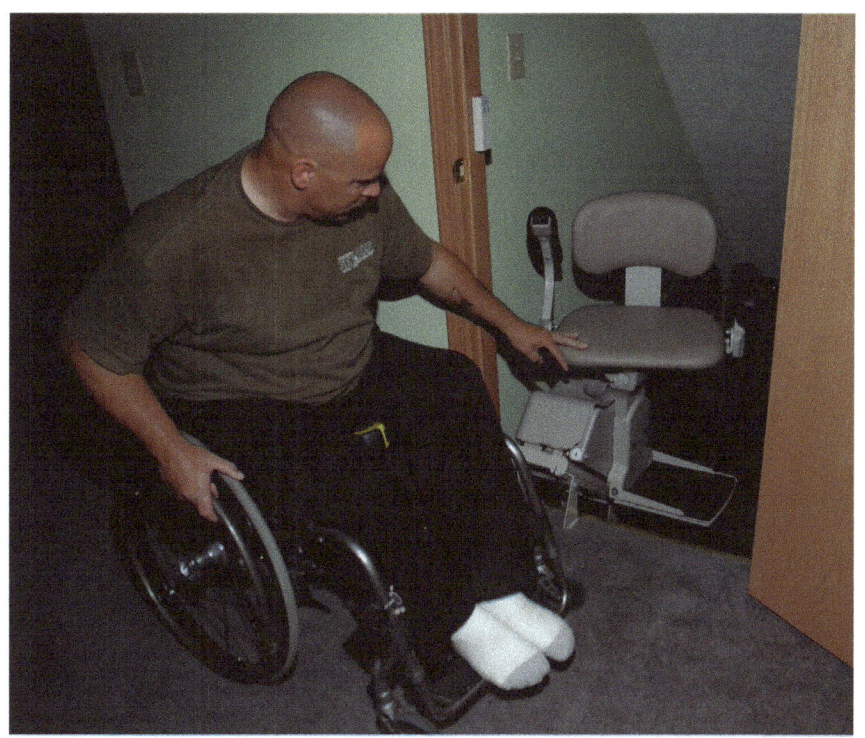
Mark Mix

"The Center for Universal Design (1997). The Principles of Universal Design, Version 2.0. Raleigh, NC: North Carolina State University."

3 TEN MYTHS ABOUT UNIVERSAL DESIGN

By Rosemarie Rossetti, Ph.D.

As I speak around the country about universal design housing, members of my audience composed of interior designers, architects, builders and consumers ask many questions. It has occurred to me over the past several years that there are many misconceptions about universal design. Let me share a few of the top myths and explain reality from my perspective.

Myth #1: A home using universal design looks ugly, institutional and stereotypes the home so people know it was designed for a person with a disability.

Reality: The beauty of a universal designed home depends on the skill and experience of the designers. Well-designed homes with universal design features and products enhance the beauty of a home while making it functional for people with disabilities, as well as convenient for people without disabilities. Universal design is for everyone, not just people with disabilities. There are many beautiful non-institutional looking universal design products, such as colored vinyl, bronze, satin nickel, and polished brass grab bars, in the marketplace. Much of a home's beauty comes from the finishes of the plumbing fixtures, appliances, hardware, cabinets, countertops, wall treatment, and flooring. Experienced and knowledgeable designers can find universal design products available in these beautiful finishes.

 Universal Design Toolkit

Myth #2: Universal design costs more due to the building design and products with universal design features, such as windows, appliances and plumbing fixtures.

Reality: My experience building my own home, the Universal Design Living Laboratory (www.UDLL.com), the national demonstration home and garden in Columbus, OH, has shown that there are many choices when it comes to selecting products for the home. Those with universal design features are not more expensive as a general rule, though early adopters have paid the price of being ahead of the current wave of appliance price reduction that occurs with more acceptance of universal design features. In fact, by adding design features and products that support universal design, the home will have more value to the occupants because it will be more usable for a lifetime.

Myth #3: Universal design takes more square footage.

Reality: Space planning is critical in home design, especially when the homeowner uses a wheelchair. As a person who uses a wheelchair, I am very cognizant of where extra space is needed and how to be conservative with space planning when creating a floor plan. By creating an open plan with fewer hallways, square footage can be conserved. By putting adequate space in the kitchen and bathrooms, there will be a lot more accessibility, comfort, and convenience. A universal design home need not have additional square footage, but rather have adequate room for a person to navigate the home from a wheelchair. Multiple uses of a space and overlap of their clear floor spaces allow relatively small rooms to include the necessary larger clear floor spaces.

 Universal Design Toolkit

Myth #4: The resale value of the home will be less due to limiting the number of buyers who would be interested in those universal design features.

Reality: Quite the opposite is true. Universal design is for a large market of people of all ages and abilities. Universal design is human-centered design. The inclusive design of spaces and products benefit people of all ages, with or without physical or mental limitations. No one can predict when a short term or long term disability will be a part of our lives. It is far better to plan for homes to accommodate us as we age rather than to be forced out of our homes when circumstances change. As the US population gets older, especially the baby boomers, they will be remaining in their homes longer. Many are opting to renovate their homes, and others are choosing additions to help them to age in their homes. Some are purchasing new homes of a smaller size than their last home. Even families with young children find universal design houses more convenient. They are all looking for features that provide safety, convenience of style for raising a family or aging in their homes. Universal design features provide for safety and add value to a home.

 Universal Design Toolkit

Myth #5: The Americans with Disabilities Act (ADA) has so many regulations that are very complicated to follow when designing homes with universal design features.

Reality: The ADA does not apply to single family housing unless federal funding was utilized. Private homeowners do not have to follow ADA criteria.

Myth #6: The builder and their subcontractors are used to doing it their way and will not follow my design properly to include universal design features. It's too hard to change their building process.

Reality: Builders are becoming certified through the National Association of Home Builders in the Certified Aging in Place Specialist program and are learning how to implement universal design principles. Builders must insist that their subcontractors read the plans and follow the procedures for building and remodeling homes. As products are ordered by the builder, the universal design features are already a part of the design. As builders construct more homes with universal design features, universal design will become the new standard in the building industry as better living design.

UDLL construction consultant Bob White (pointing)

 Universal Design Toolkit

Myth #7: A home containing universal design features will be harder to pass a building code inspection.

Reality: By the very nature and definition of universal design, there are no practices that go against federal and state building codes. There are usually provisions for local variances should a question arise in the plan review stage.

Myth #8: Universal design homes have ramps at the front door causing the home to be labeled as a home for a person with a disability.

Reality: For existing homes, in order to create a no step entrance, there are some instances where a ramp at the front door is the only solution; in others, modifying the grade around the home may be the best solution. All new properties and most existing homes can be designed with a no step entrance. Also, ramps in the garage, side door, or rear door are usually not visible from the street.

Myth #9: Universal design is restricted to building a ranch style home.

Reality: First floor living is the goal for universal design, however, multilevel homes can also be constructed with provisions for access to the upper and lower floors by way of elevators, platform lifts and stair lifts.

 Universal Design Toolkit

Myth #10: Universal design is just another name for handicap accessibility.

Reality: Accessibility is about compliance with regulations and building codes. Universal design is about creating environments that give people flexibility, choices and options in how they use those environments. Accessibility is often a starting point for universal design, which goes beyond access to empower people.

Beth Bookwalter at home elevator entrance

GLOSSARY OF TERMS RELATED TO UNIVERSAL DESIGN

Accessible Design

Meets the prescribed Americans with Disabilities Act requirements or other mandatory requirements found in state, local, and model building codes. The ADA requirements do not apply on single family privately funded homes. Generally, accessible design achieves functional solutions for people with disabilities (i.e. mobility limitations) or with extreme human performance characteristics (i.e. height and weight). Homes with accessible design have features that generally accommodate a resident with a disability. An example of an accessible design feature is a 9" X 6" toe kick under a base cabinet. This provides room for the feet and foot rest of a person who uses a wheelchair. Also, installing a grab bar would qualify as an accessible design feature.

Adaptable Design

Includes features in the home that can be readily adjusted or adapted in a short period of time using unskilled labor and not involving structural or finished material changes. An example of an adaptable design feature is a closet rod that can be raised or lowered with a few hand tools.

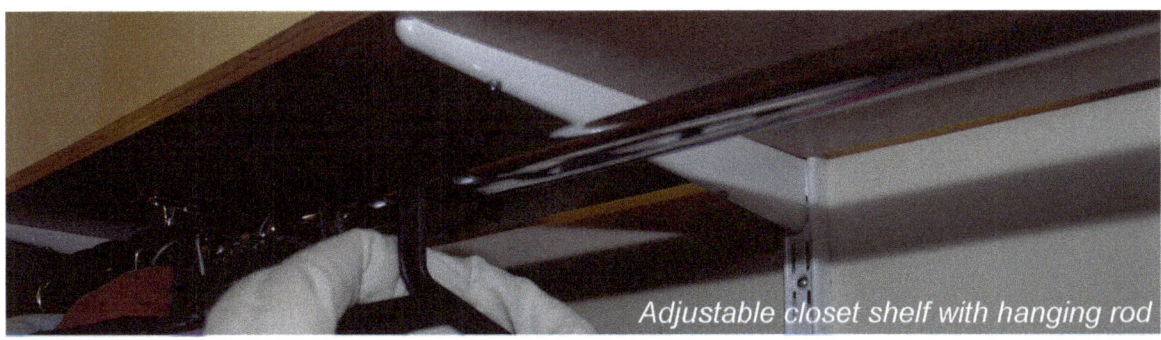

Adjustable closet shelf with hanging rod

Universal Design Toolkit

Design for All

Is design tailored to human diversity. Design for All is the intervention into environments, products and services which aims to ensure that anyone, including future generations, regardless of age, gender, capacities or cultural background, can participate in social, economic, cultural and leisure activities with equal opportunities.

Aging in Place

The ability to live in one's own home and community safely, independently, and comfortably, regardless of age, income or ability level.

Human-Centered Design

Human-centered design is a creative approach to problem solving. It's a process that starts with the people you're designing for and ends with new solutions that are tailor made to suit their needs. Human-centered design is all about building a deep empathy with the people you're designing for; generating tons of ideas; building a bunch of prototypes; sharing what you've made with the people you're designing for; and eventually putting your innovative new solution out in the world.

Human-centered design consists of three phases. In the Inspiration Phase you'll learn directly from the people you're designing for as you immerse yourself in their lives and come to deeply understand their needs. In the Ideation Phase you'll make sense of what you learned, identify opportunities for design, and prototype possible solutions. And in the Implementation Phase you'll bring your solution to life, and eventually, to market. And you'll know that your solution will be a success because you've kept the very people you're looking to serve at the heart of the process.

Inclusive Design

Every design decision has the potential to include or exclude customers. Inclusive design emphasizes the contribution that understanding user diversity makes to informing these decisions, and thus to including as many people as possible. User diversity covers variation in capabilities, needs, and aspirations. Inclusive design does not suggest that it is always possible (or appropriate) to design one product to address the needs of the entire population. Instead, inclusive design guides an appropriate design response to diversity in the population through:

- Developing a family of products and derivatives to provide the best possible coverage of the population.

- Ensuring that each individual product has clear and distinct target users.

- Reducing the level of ability required to use each product, in order to improve the user experience for a broad range of customers, in a variety of situations.

Universal Design

The design of products, environments, and communication to be usable by all people, to the greatest extent possible, without adaptation or specialized design. The concept is also called inclusive design, design-for-all, lifespan design or human-centered design.

Casement window with crank

 Universal Design Toolkit

Visitability

An international movement to change home construction practices so that new homes offer three specific accessibility features. To learn more, go to http://www.visitability.org

- At least one zero-step entrance at the front, back or side of the house on an accessible route leading from a driveway or public sidewalk.

- All main floor doors, including bathrooms, with at least 32 inches of clear passage space.

- At least a half bathroom on the main floor that is wheelchair accessible.

See Also:

"**Definitions: Accessible. Adaptable, and Universal Design**", The Center for Universal Design, North Carolina State University, 2006

https://www.ncsu.edu/www/ncsu/design/sod5/cud/pubs_p/docs/Fact%20Sheet%206.pdf

Ramp entrance from garage

IMPORTANT SPACE PLANNING DIMENSIONS FOR PEOPLE WHO USE WHEELCHAIRS OR WALKERS

Design for the person and the mobility device that person is using and may use in the future as they age. Manual wheelchairs, power wheelchairs, scooters and walkers are available in a variety of sizes. Allocate the space for movement and maneuvering.

ANTHROPOMETRICS

(The dimensions of the human body) for an average adult in a wheelchair:

- **Average wheelchair seat height**

    20" high from the floor. Impacts the ease of transferring to and from a wheelchair.

- **Eye level**

    41 - 48" high from the floor. Impacts window sill height, thermostat placement.

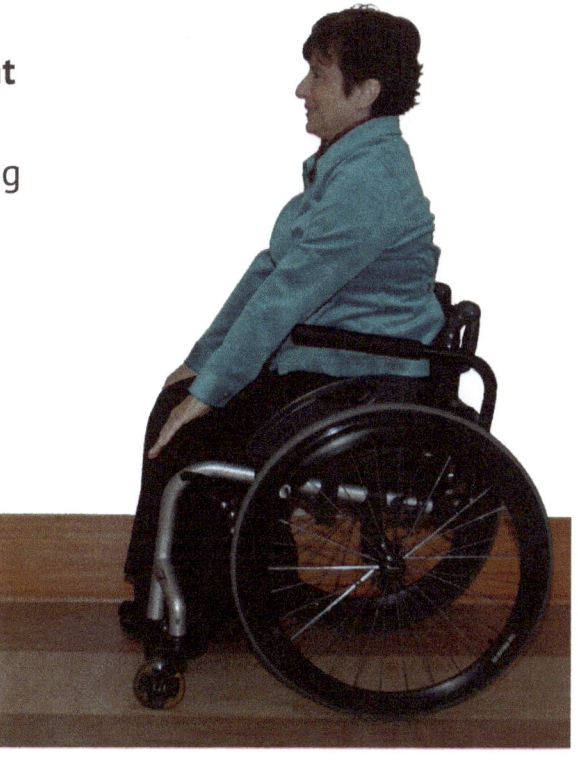

DIMENSIONS

ANTHROPOMETRICS

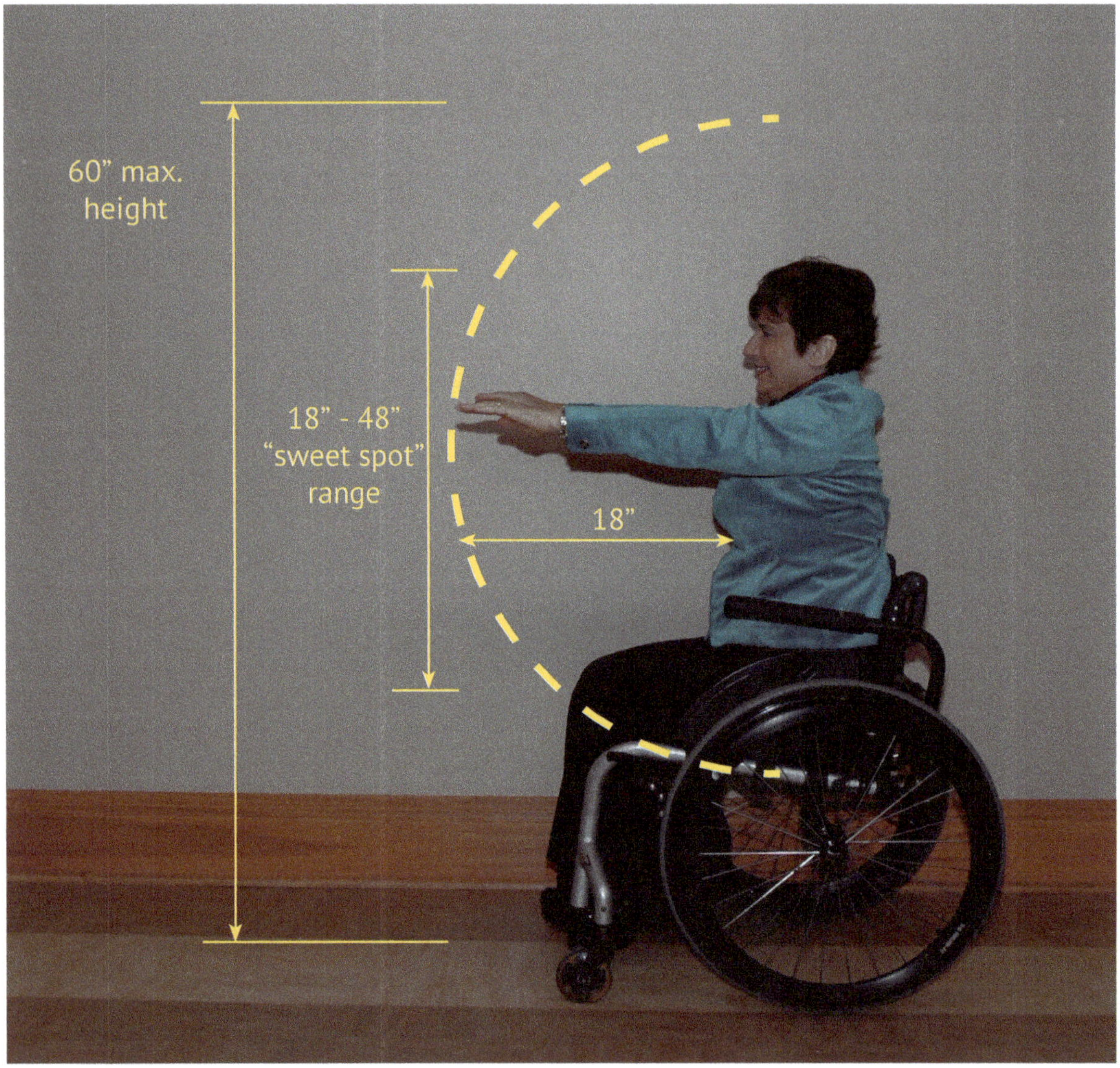

- **Forward reach vertical range**

Forward lean may not be an option for some individuals. Leaning allows additional reach, but may affect balance.

Impacts heights for:

- ☐ shelves, drawers and clothing rods
- ☐ operation of appliances and electronics

Universal Design Toolkit

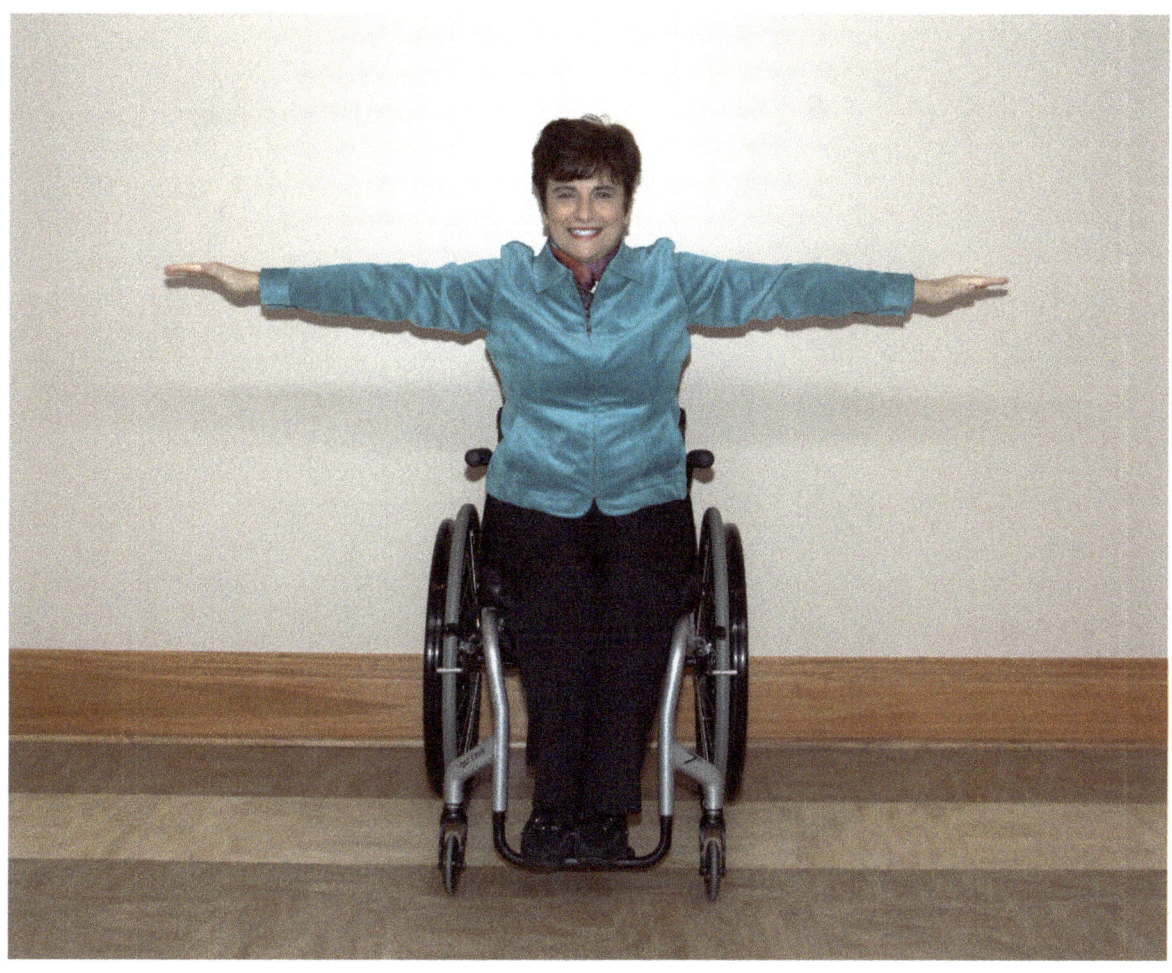

- **Side reach range**
Average 14" to 24" from wheelchair rim to fingertips
Useful for:

    ☐ retrieval / placement of objects

    ☐ pushing / pulling (doors / drawers)

Not an ideal position for performing tasks (in front of sinks, cooktops, etc).

DIMENSIONS

TURNING — 360°

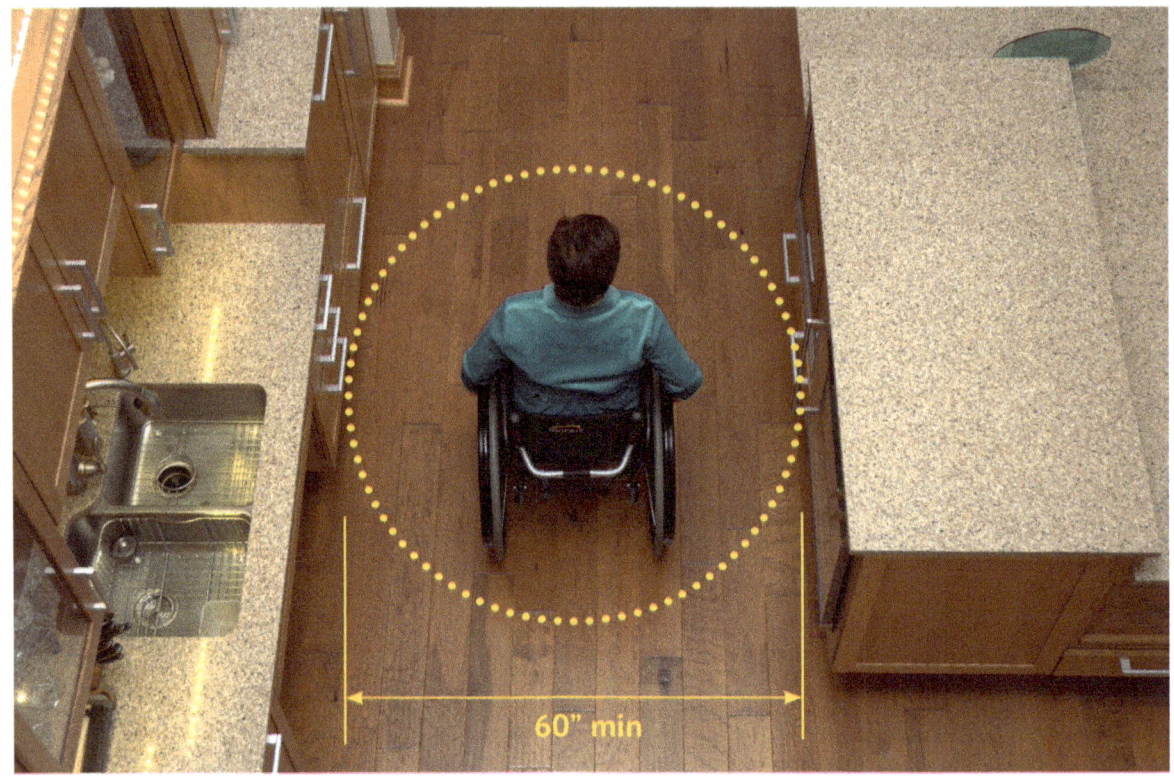

- **Turning diameter**

  60" (5 feet) for a wheelchair to make a complete circle turn throughout the home.

- A person using a large wheelchair, walker or scooter may require 72" (6 feet) or even 84" (7 feet) for a turning diameter.

DIMENSIONS

Universal Design Toolkit

TURNING — T-TURN - 180°

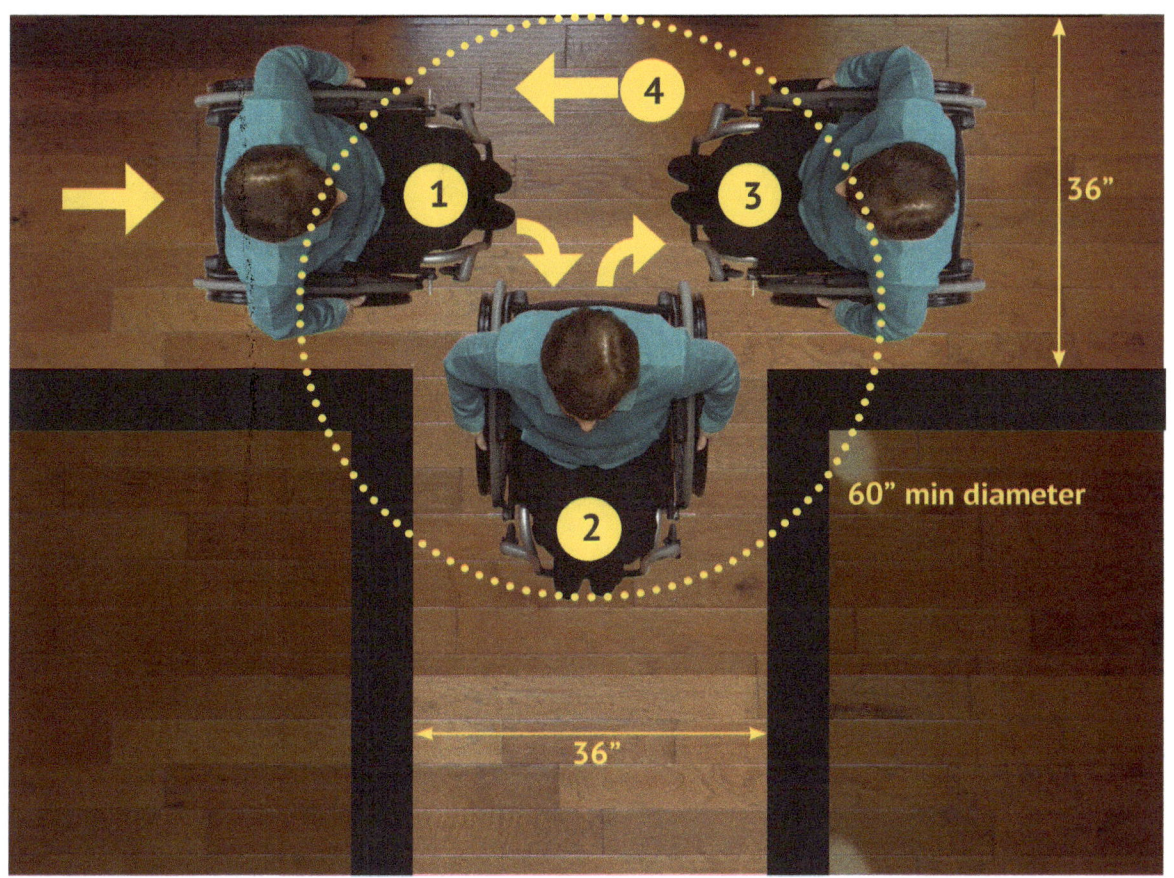

- **T-Turn**

    36" X 36" X 72" space is required for a wheelchair to make a 180° T-turn when a full 60" diameter space is not available.

    Increase the T-turn dimensions for a power or large size wheelchairs.

DIMENSIONS

 Universal Design Toolkit

SPACE FOR VEHICLE

- **Side door wheelchair accessible van (ramp or lift):**

  - ☐ 2-1/2 car garage, based on 16 foot garage door width. Must allow space for ramp fold down and 60" diameter chair maneuvering beyond ramp. Same dimensions apply if parking outdoors.

  - ☐ If van has height extension cap, garage door and garage area height must be increased.

- **Rear entry wheelchair accessible van (ramp):**

  - ☐ 5 feet additional space required at rear of van for fold-out ramp and 60" diameter chair maneuvering beyond ramp (10 feet total additional length).

  - ☐ 2 car garage width desirable to allow individual to maneuver into the garage alongside the van.

  - ☐ If parking outdoors, allow additional side space (48") for wheelchair or walker to travel alongside the van.

DIMENSIONS

Universal Design Toolkit

RAMPS

Lawcain Photography / Dreamstime

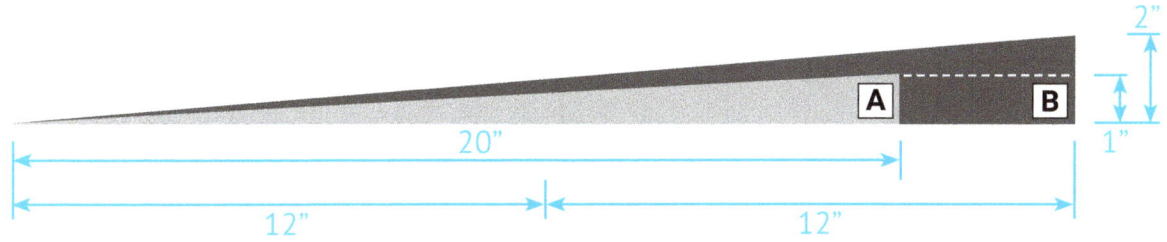

- **Ramps** should be built with as minimal slope as possible. Two ramp slopes are shown in the diagram above:

  - **Ramp "A":** 1:20 (for every 20" of distance, there is 1" of rise). Railings are not required for this ramp slope. Anything greater than this requires handrails.

  - **Ramp "B":** 1:12 (for every 12" of distance, there is 1" of rise). This steeper ramp is the maximum slope allowed by ADA.

  - Curbs should be installed along ramp edges to prevent wheelchair wheels and walker tips from slipping off.

  - Refer to this tool to calculate slopes. www.archtoolbox.com/measurements/geometry/slope.html

DIMENSIONS

WINDOWS

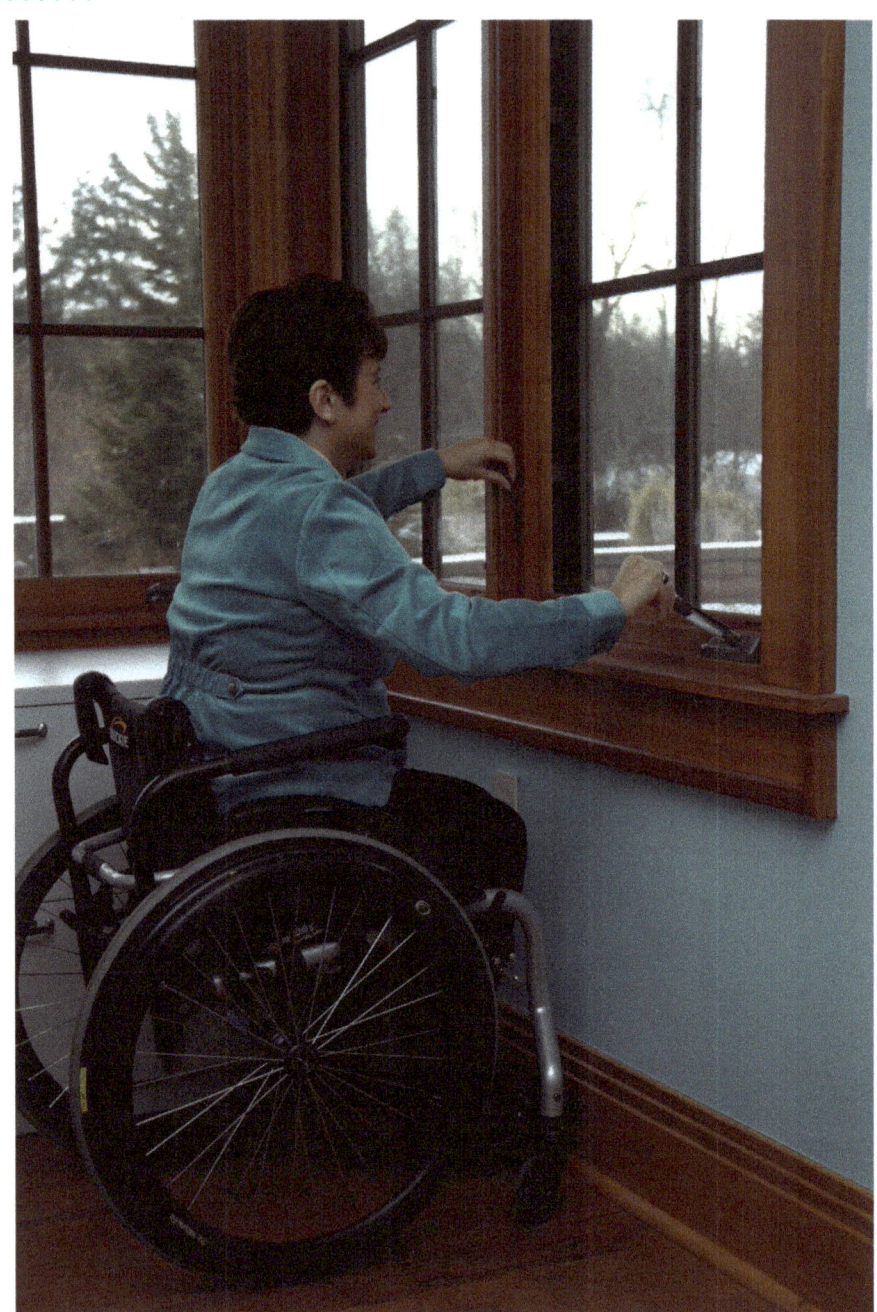

- **Window sill height** – windows used for viewing should have a window sill no higher than 36".

- Casement windows (shown) with crank and low mounted single lever lock for easy operating from a seated position.

DIMENSIONS

Universal Design Toolkit

DOOR WIDTH

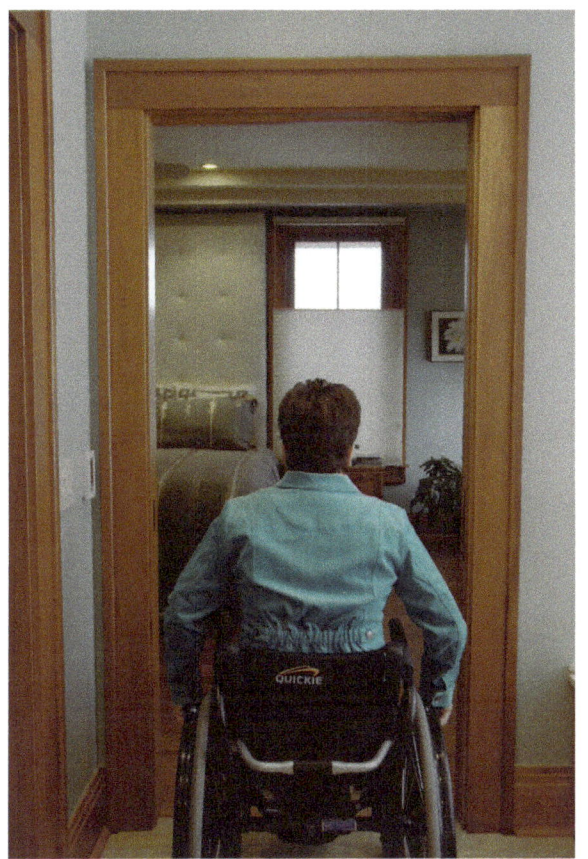
Pocket Door

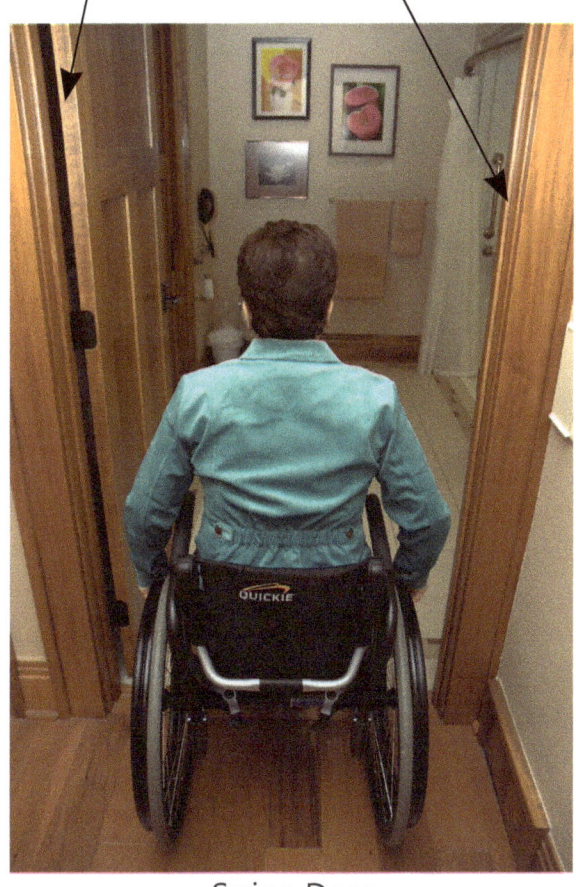
Swing Door

- **Door width** – minimum opening clearance of 32" wide. Prefer 36" wide doors. Large wheelchairs, scooters, and walkers could require could require 42" wide doors for proper clearance.

  - ☐ **36" swing door clearances:**
    - 35-1/4" between jamb stops
    - 33-7/8" between open door and jamb stop
  - ☐ **36" pocket door clearance:** 35" (no jamb stops needed)

DIMENSIONS

DOOR SWING

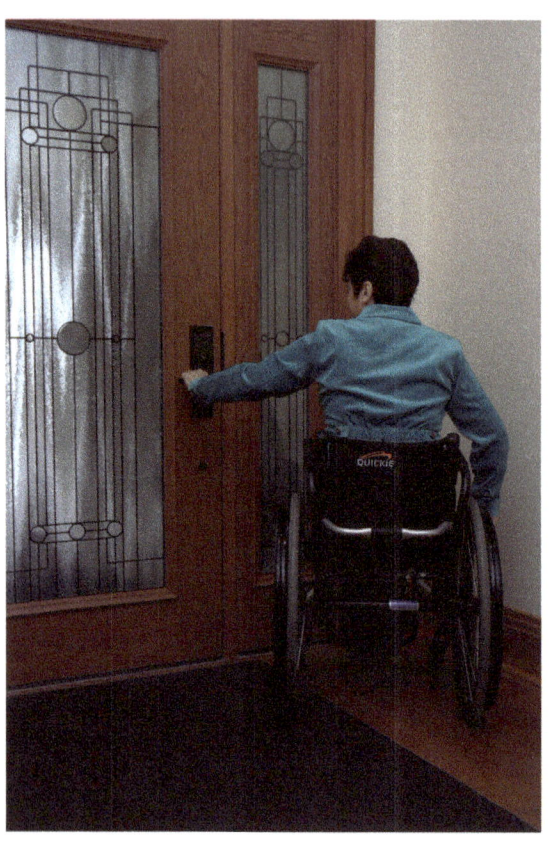
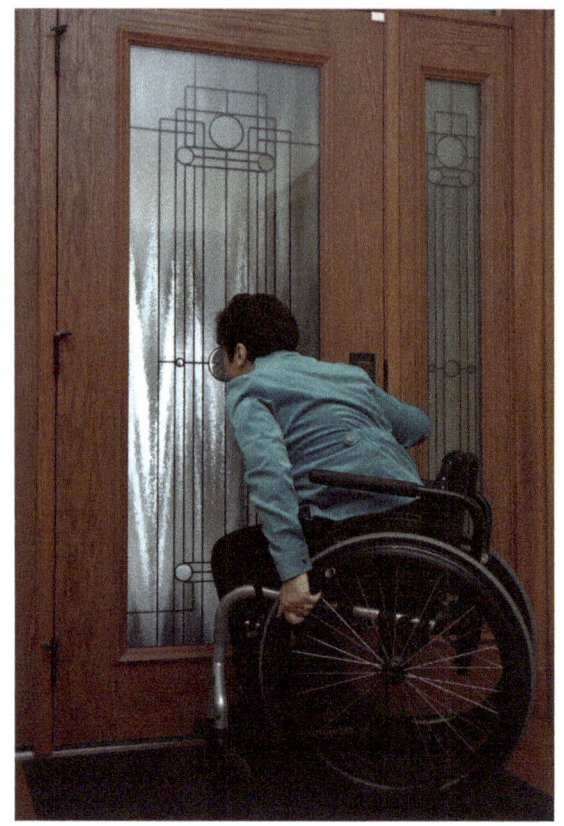

- **Door swing –** provide 18 -24" space on the latch side where a door swings toward you.

- **Provide a peephole** at 43" above the floor for a seated person. A peephole can also be installed at a standard 60" height above the floor.

- Interior doors should swing OUT from a closed room (such as a bath). This makes it much easier for help to get to a fallen person blocking the door.

THRESHOLDS

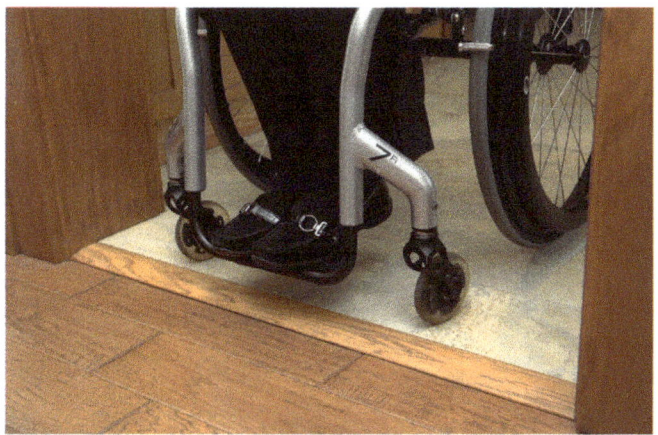

- Interior threshold strip (wood) which transitions two floor surfaces of unequal heights.

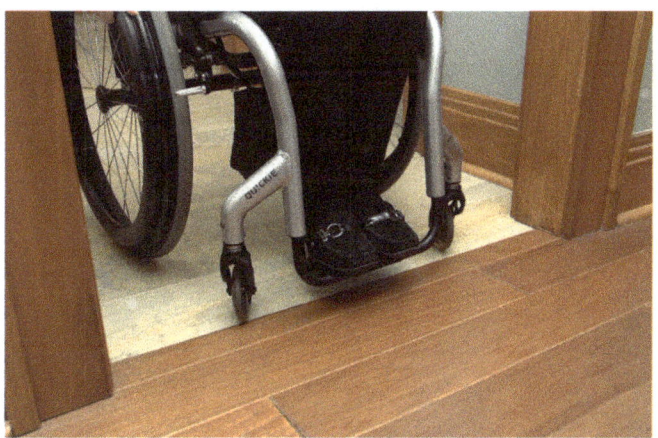

- Interior flooring surfaces of equal height do not need a transiton strip. In this instance, the wood flooring was raised slightly by placing / feathering floor fill underneath.

- Entry door aluminum threshold, 1/2" maximum height.

- **Thresholds –** 1/4" to 1/2" maximum height with beveled sides.

HALLWAYS

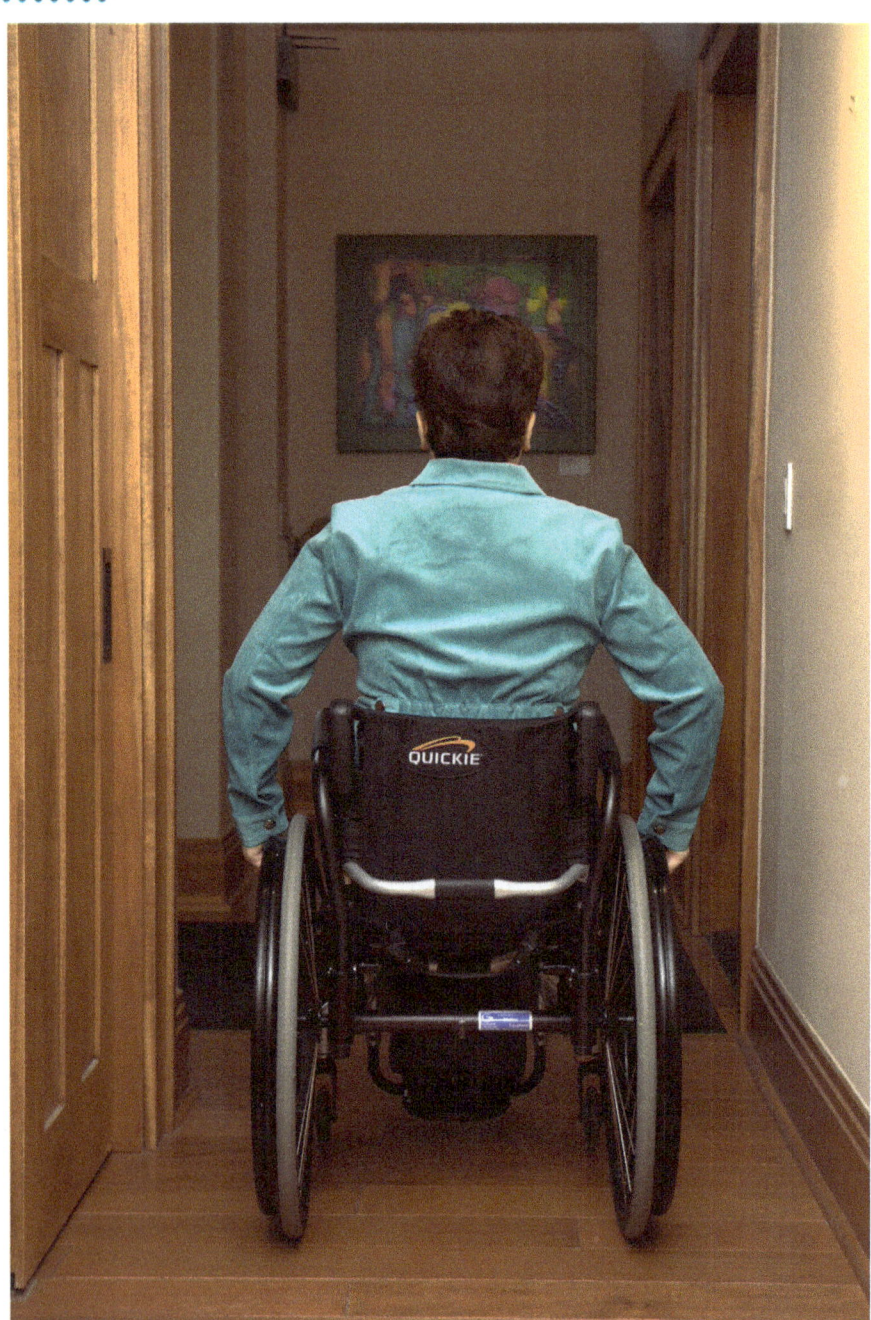

DIMENSIONS

- **Hallway width** – minimum 42", prefer 48" wide.
- Install railings if hallway is more than 6' long. Mount 34" to 38" above the floor (adjust for occupant need).

Universal Design Toolkit

BEDROOM

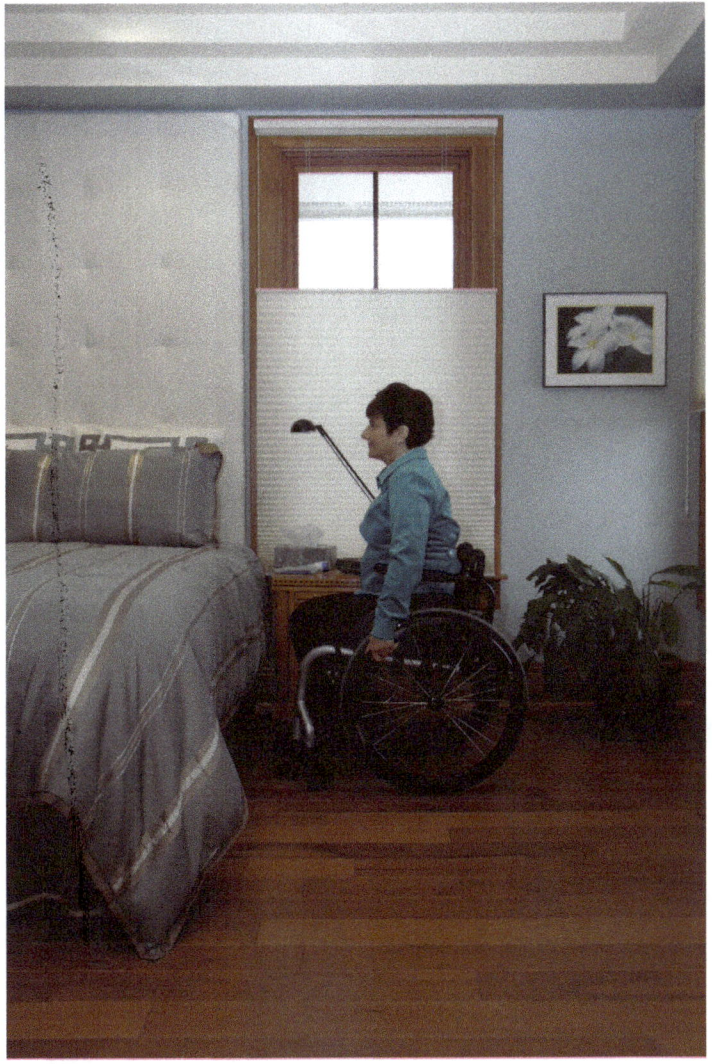

- **Bed placement –** allow 36" on each side of the bed and 42" at the foot of the bed for approach, transfer and maintenance.

- **Consider installing blocking and bracing** in the ceiling framing area over the bed and along a path of travel to the bath. This inexpensive pre-planning now will permit easy installation of a track type motorized lift / assist system in the future.

- Attempt to minimize the height difference between the bed and the wheelchair seat for easier transfer.

DIMENSIONS

ELEVATOR & STAIRS

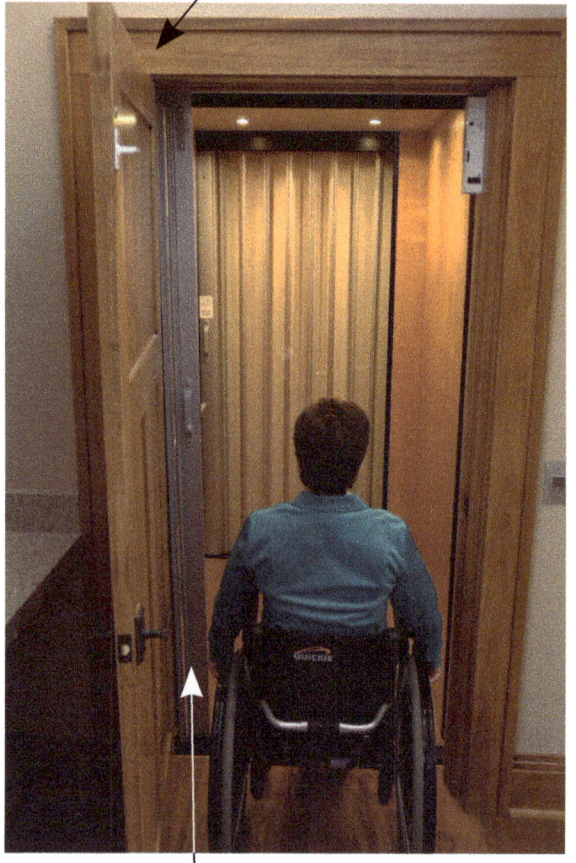
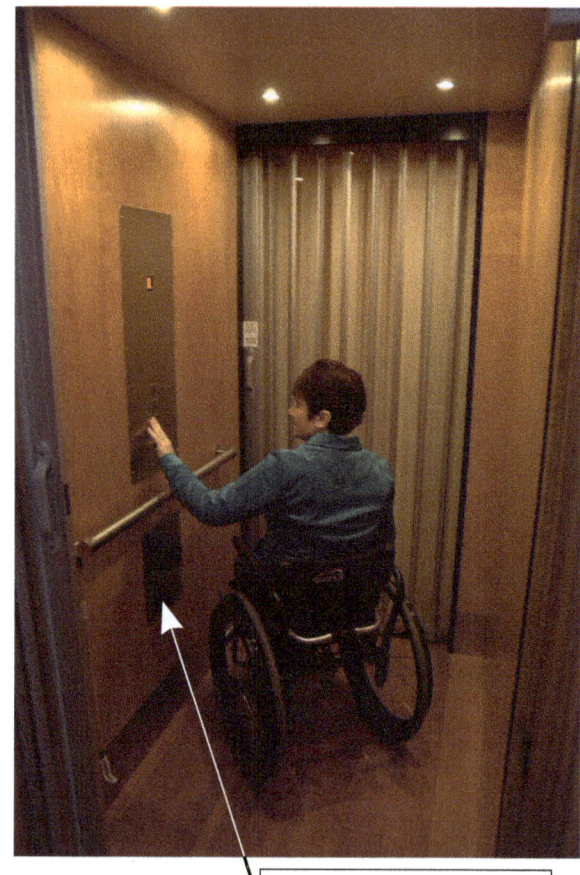

Automatic door closer mounting position for swing door

Accordian cab door

Wired phone (required by code)

- **Elevator car size** – minimum 3' X 4'. Car size is dependent on the size of the wheelchair or walker and the number of people that will need to be in the elevator at one time.

- Be aware of the cab interior door (silver accordian in the photos). This door may reduce the entry and exit width.

- **Automatic door closers** can be added to the swing-type entry doors.

- Allow 18" - 24" approach on the latch side of the swing door.

Universal Design Toolkit

ELEVATOR & STAIRS

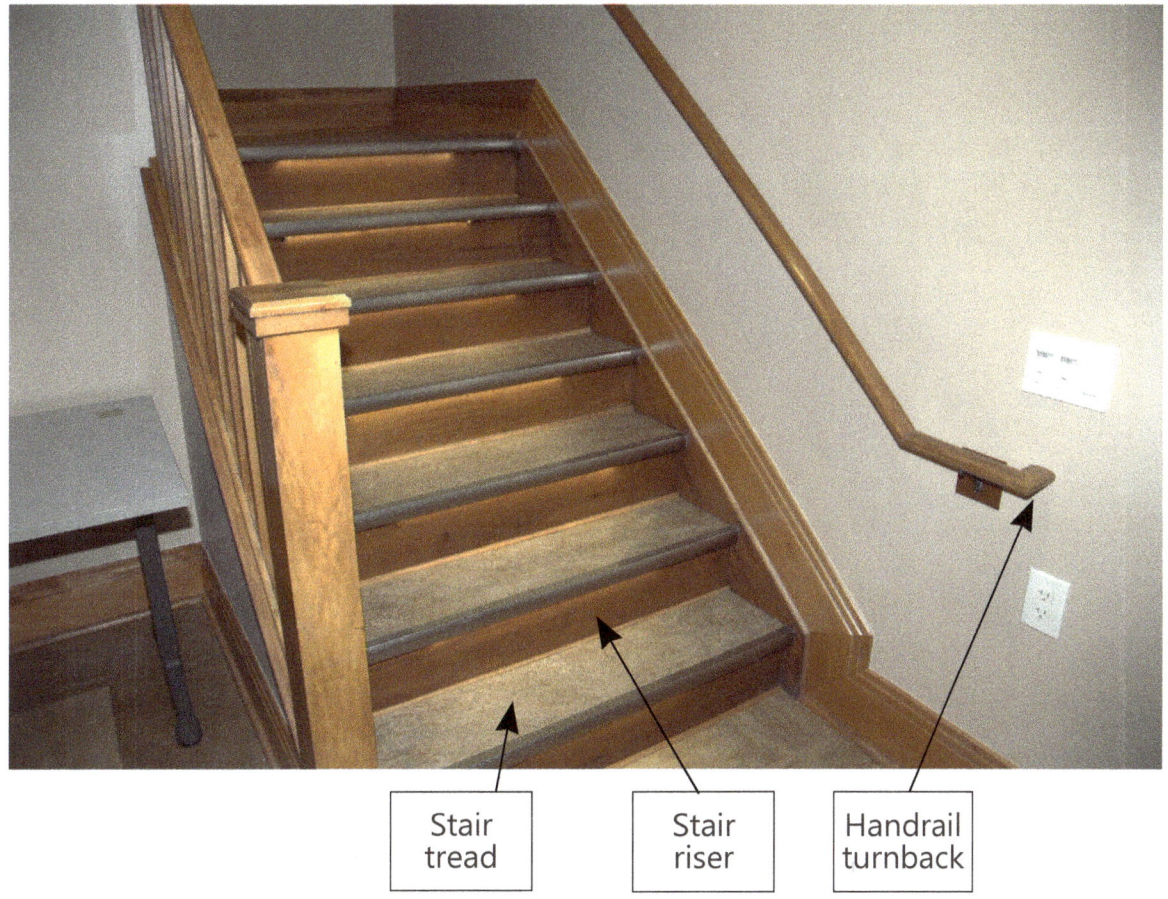

Stair tread | Stair riser | Handrail turnback

- **Stairs** will need a width of 42" to 48" to accommodate a stair lift.

- **Handrails** should be on both sides of the stairs, and should extend 12" beyond the last step. Mount rails 34" to 38" above the tread. Wall mounted handrails should have turnbacks at the ends to prevent snagging of clothing. Mount brackets to solid blocking / studs.

- **Install an electrical outlet** at top and bottom of the stairs to facilitate a future stair lift installation.

- **Contrasting colors of the stair** "riser" (dark brown in photo), and the stair tread (lighter brown) make steps easier to see.

- **Lighted stair treads** using LED tape enhance visability and safety.

DIMENSIONS

ELECTRICAL & CONTROLS

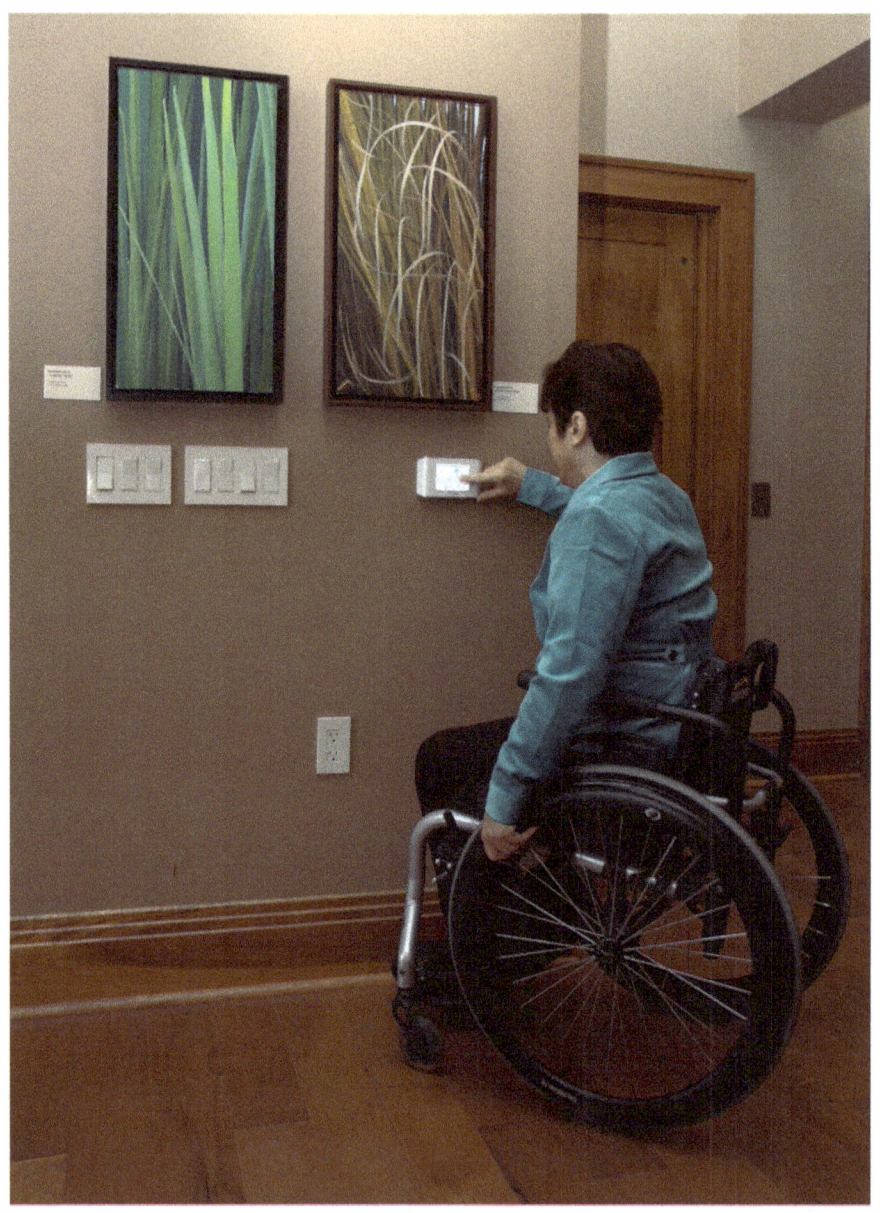

- **Light switch height –** 42" from the floor to the center of the switch. Any controls, such as thermostats, should be mounted at this height too.

- **Electrical outlet height –** 20" minimum (24" preferred) from the floor to the center of the outlet.

Universal Design Toolkit

ELECTRICAL & CONTROLS

- **Electrical circuit breaker panels** should be mounted within easy reach of a seated person. In this instance, the top breaker is 54" above the floor.

- The breaker panels are located in the ground floor garage, instead of a basement area. The makes the panels much more accessible and safer than going to a basement area.

# Universal Design Toolkit

BATH VANITY

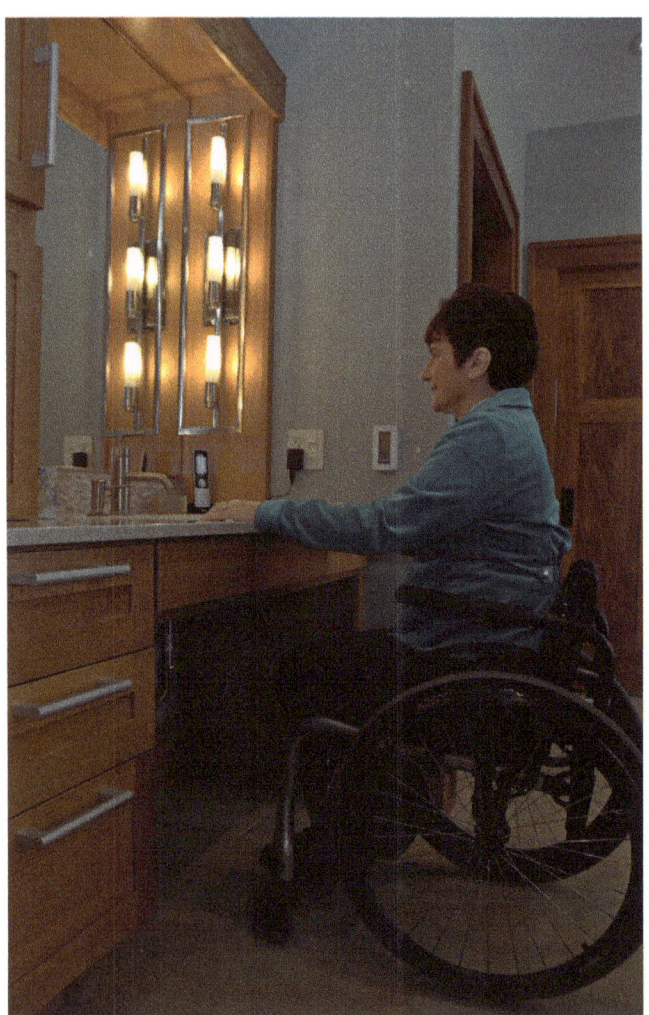

- **Countertop:** 32" high from the floor preferred. Maximum 34"

- **Knee space height under sink:** 27" high minimum. 29" high or greater is preferred to allow clearance for wheelchair armrests.

- **Depth of knee space:** 19"

- **Width of the knee space:** 30"- 36".

- Pad the pipes underneath or install a protective panel.

DIMENSIONS

3D perspective cutaway view of a bath vanity

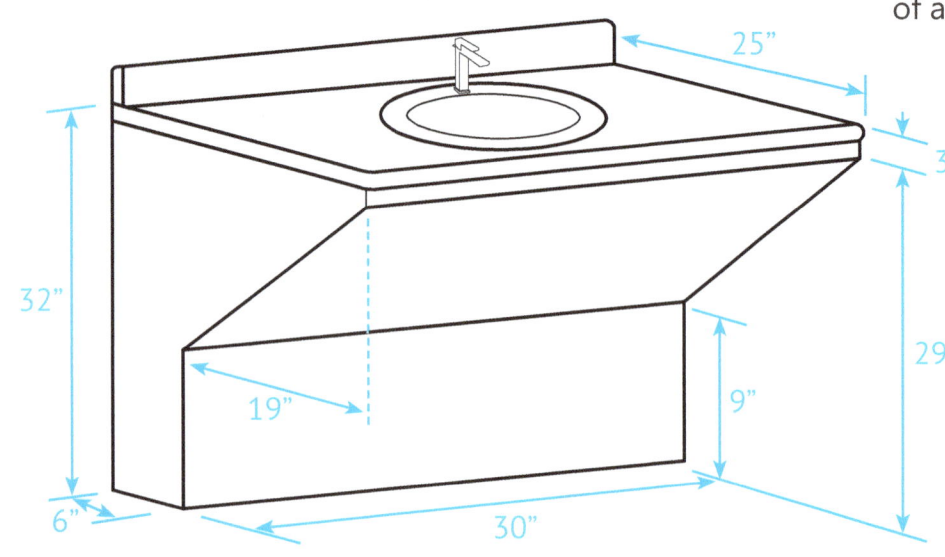

Universal Design Toolkit

BATH VANITY

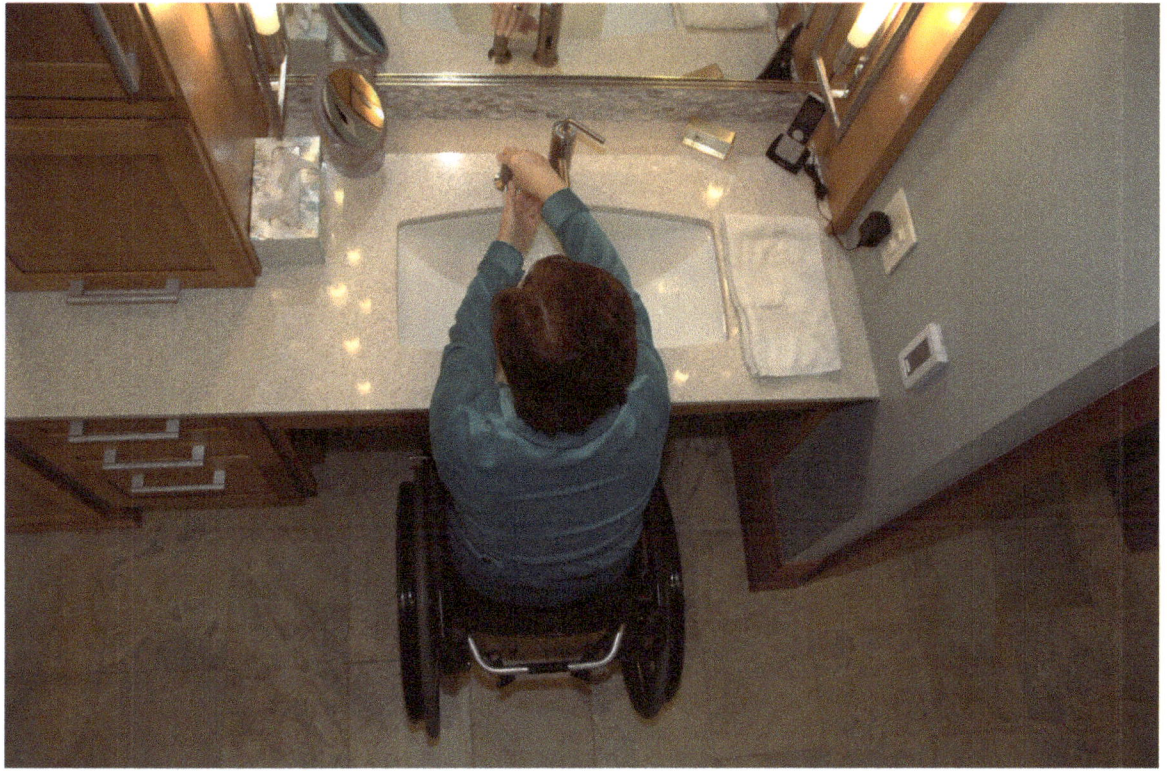

- **Consider reach and the space around the vanity area.**
  - ☐ Design the countertop to be large enough to accommodate products and accessories.
  - ☐ Install electrical outlets, light switches and other electronic controls within easy reach.
- **Approach**
  30" X 48" minimum approach *in front of* the sink.

DIMENSIONS

 Universal Design Toolkit

BATH VANITY

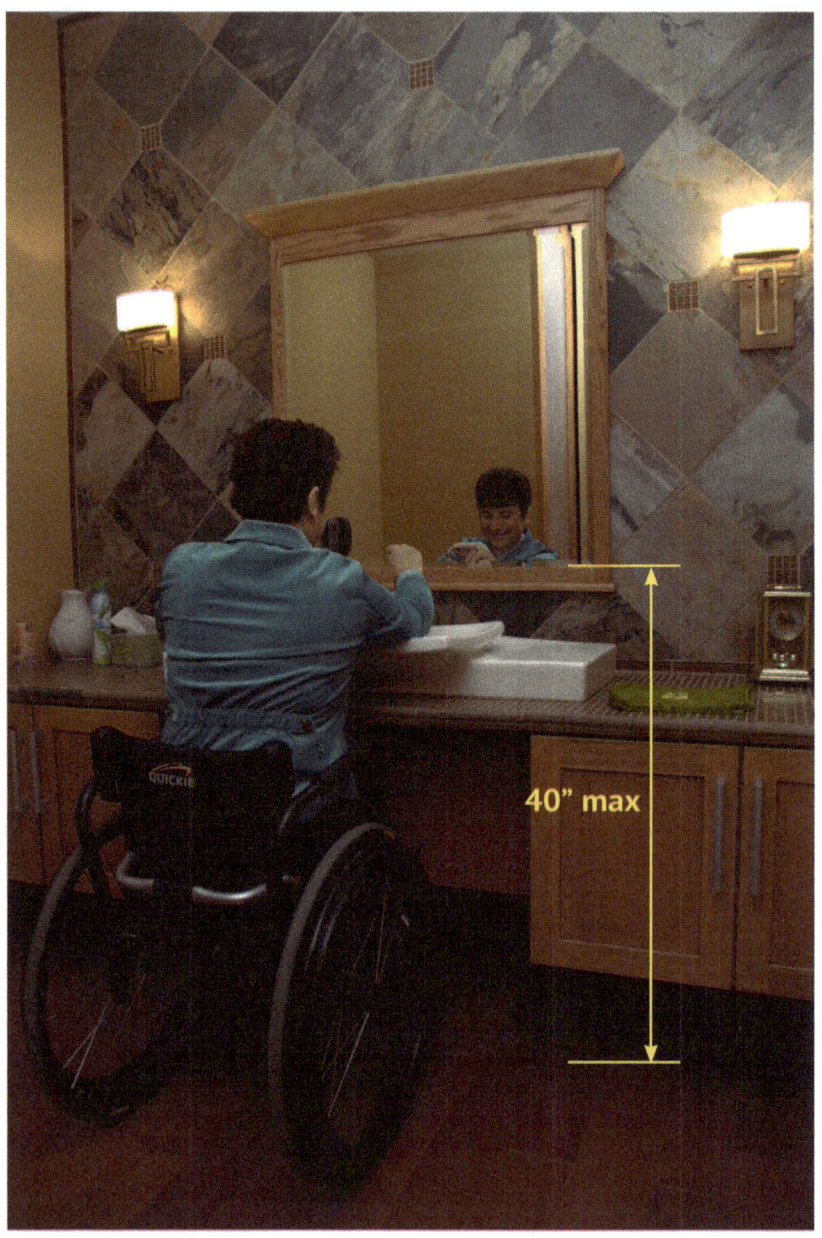

DIMENSIONS

- **Mirror height** – no higher than 40" from the floor to the bottom of the mirror and preferably at 36". Full length mirrors are recommended too.

Universal Design Toolkit

TOILETING AREA

- **Toilet height** – 17" to 18" from the floor to the top of the toilet seat

- **Toilet paper holder** – with a center line 8"-12" in front of the front edge of the toilet and 26" above the floor.

- **Grab bar placement** – Varies on the needs of the person who uses them. Could be mounted horizontally, vertically, or at an angle. Could also be added behind toilet. Typically installed 33"-36" from the floor.

DIMENSIONS

 **Universal Design Toolkit**

TOILETING AREA

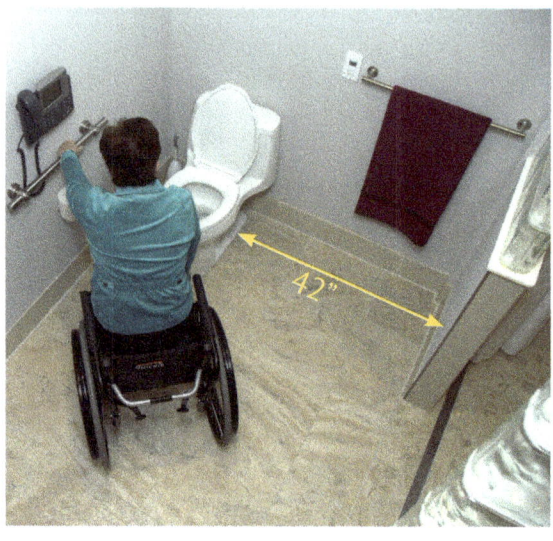 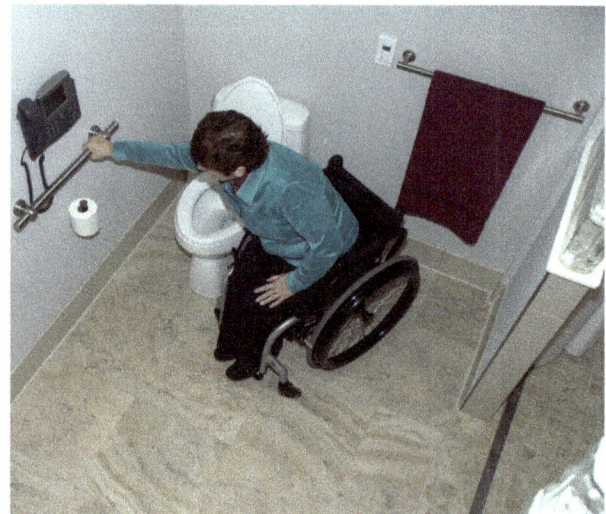

- **Approach**

  30" wide X 48" deep minimum approach *in front of* the toilet.

- **Side Clearance**

  The ADA suggests a turning diameter of 60" as measured from the front side of the toilet bowl to an adjacent wall. However, this may not be practical or needed in many residential applications.

  Rosemarie approaches the toilet straight in, holds on to the grab bar, stand and pivots (left photo).

  To position aside the toilet, a user could perform a 180° T-Turn in the room using the shower entrance. Or they could back into the toilet room.

DIMENSIONS

SHOWERING AREA

- **Curbless shower** large enough for the person to transfer from their wheelchair to a shower chair or bench.

    ☐ Minimum size: 36''' X 48"

    ☐ Preferred sizes: 36" X 60", 48" X 60", and 60" X 60" to accommodate space for an assistant to help in the transfer.

- **Sloped floor with continuous channel drain**, facilitates stable footing for wheelchairs and walkers. Water moves quickly to the drain, promoting safety.

- **Shower and controls within each reach**

- **Grab bar placement** – Varies on the needs of the person who uses them. Could be mounted horizontally, vertically, or at an angle. Typically installed 33"-36" from the floor.

Universal Design Toolkit

SHOWERING AREA

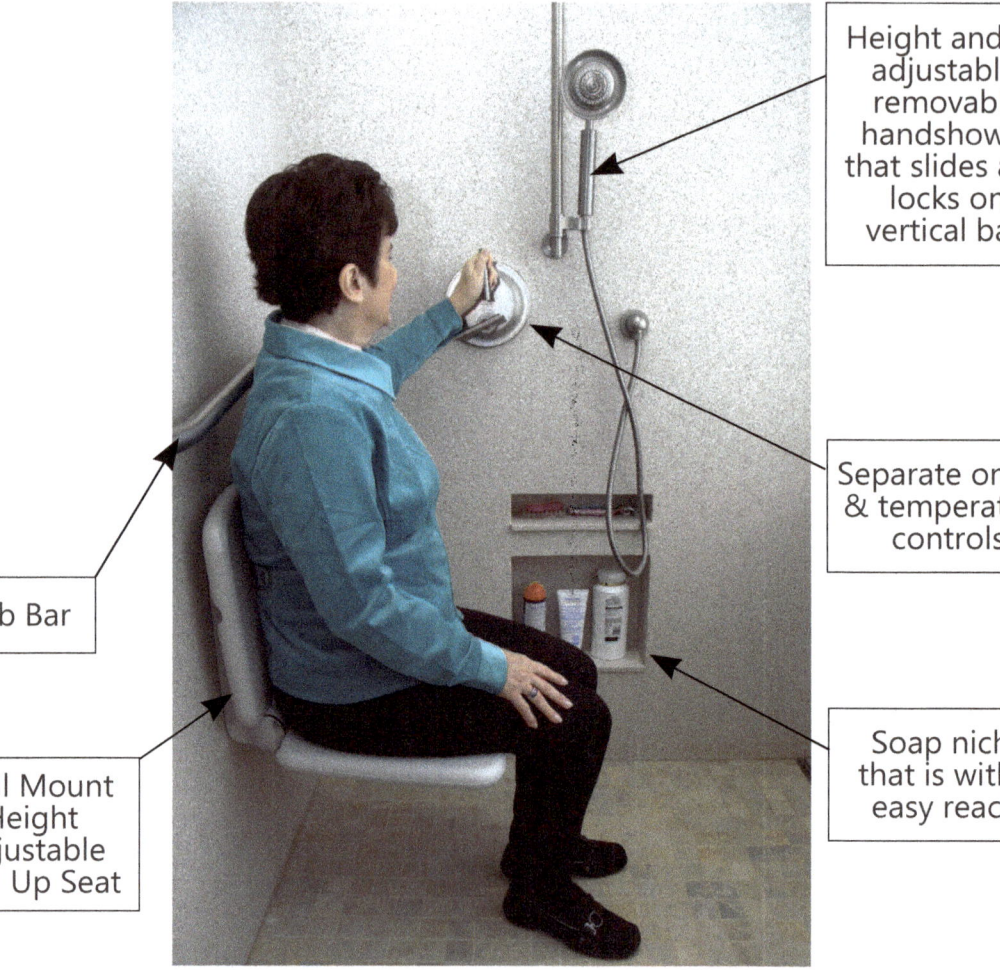

DIMENSIONS

- **Shower bench** – minimum of 18" deep by 24" wide.

- **Handshower handle grip lowest mounting point** - 45" to 55" above the floor

- **Plumbing controls mounting height** - 43" from the floor to the center of the controls.

- **Install floor tile that is slip resistant,** having a wet dynamic coefficient of friction ≥ 0.42.

SHOWERING AREA

Rosemarie has enough strength and mobility that she is able to transfer from her wheelchair to the shower chair without assistance. When showering, towels are placed on the wheelchair seat. Once seated on the shower chair, she unlocks and pushes the wheelchair out of the showering area in the doorway of the curbless shower, and then locks the wheels.

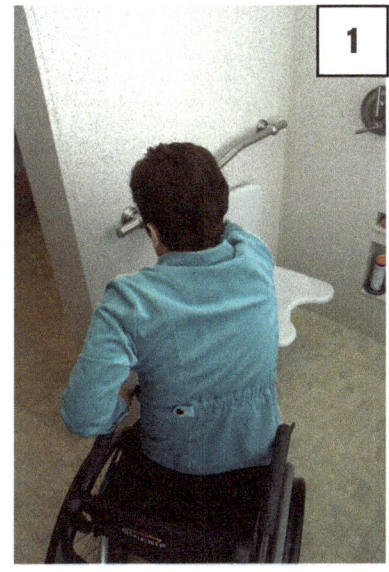
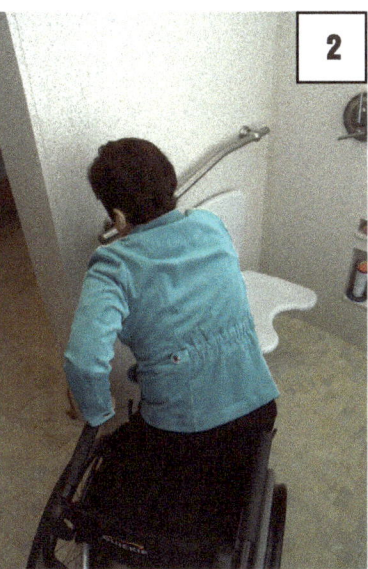
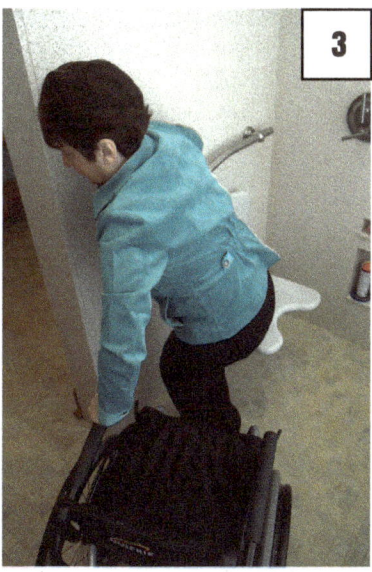
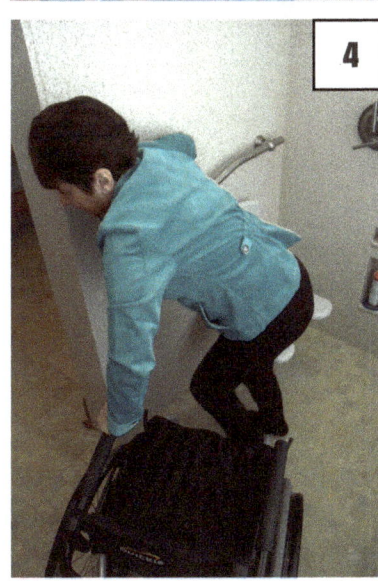

KITCHEN

DIMENSIONS

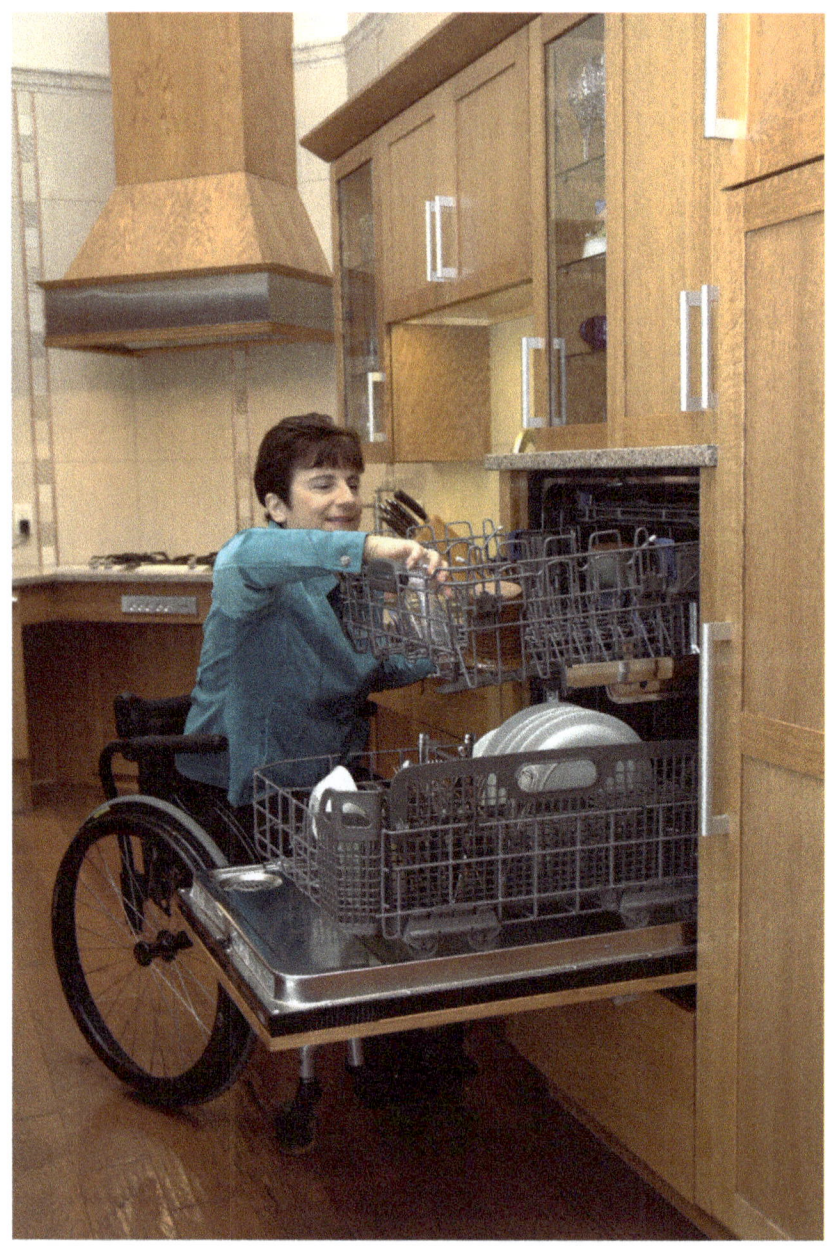

- **The dishwasher should be raised** 8" – 18" from the floor to make it easier for loading and unloading dishes.
  - ☐ Storage space can be built in under the dishwasher.

KITCHEN — WALL STORAGE

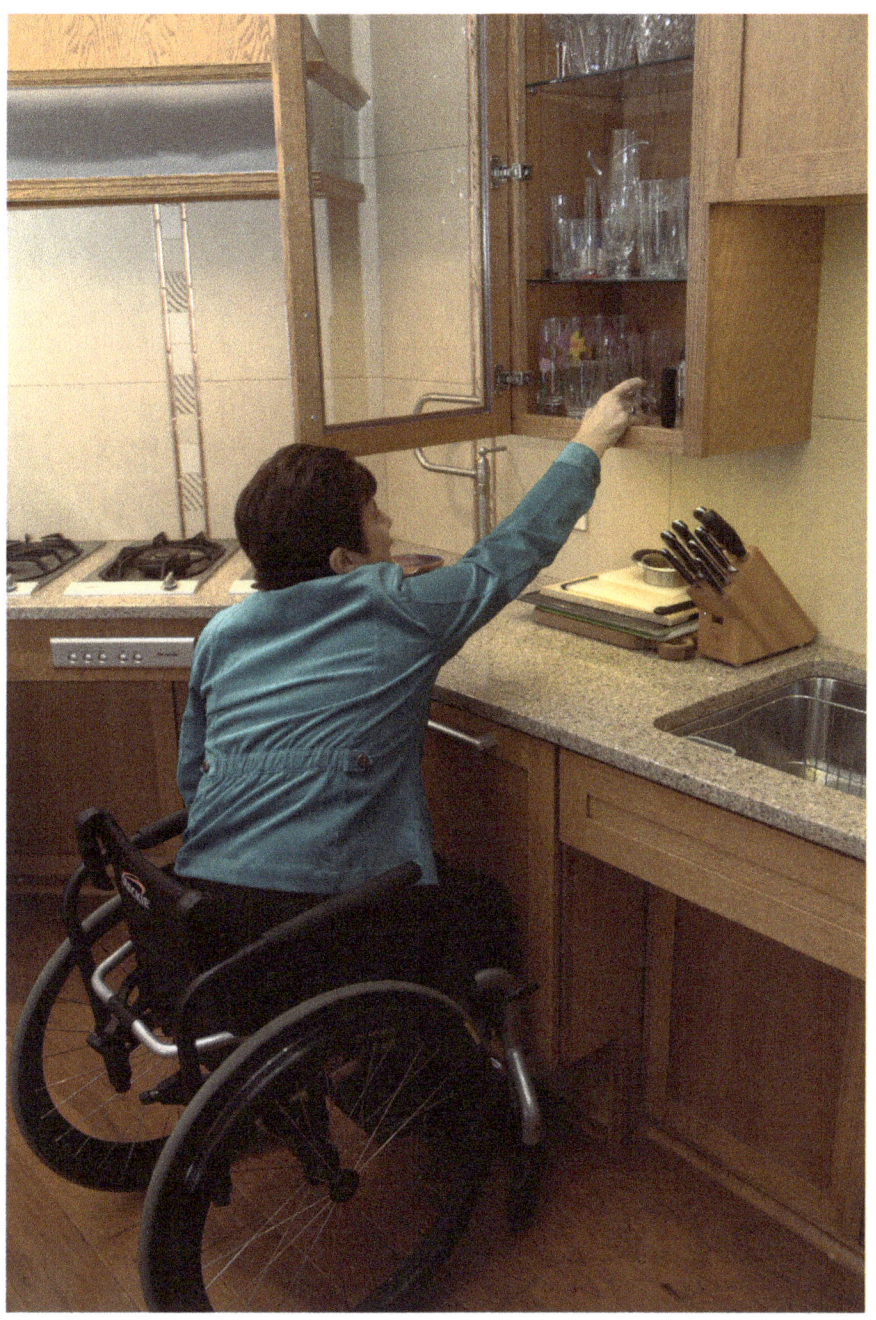

- **Kitchen wall cabinets** can be installed so the bottom of the cabinets are 14" above the countertop (instead of the traditional 18" spacing). This provides better access for people who use wheelchairs to reach the bottom shelf of the wall cabinets.

 Universal Design Toolkit

KITCHEN — COUNTERTOPS

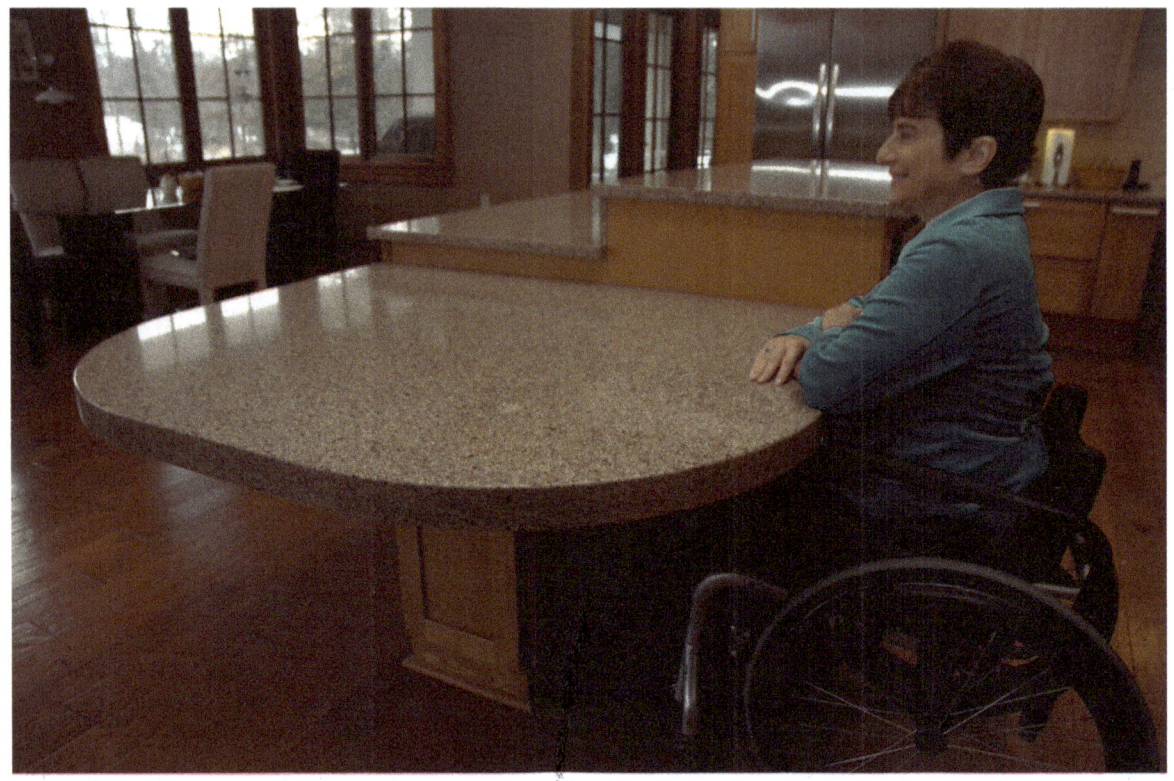

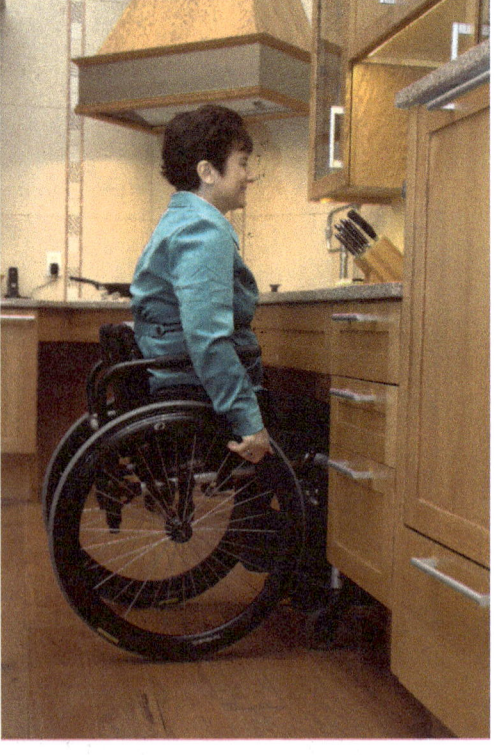

DIMENSIONS

- **Countertop heights, island** (above)
  - ☐ 30" above the floor for the half round, serves as a dining area and for food preparation.
  - ☐ 35" and 40" heights (rear two sections of the island) accomodates standing persons of various heights comfortably.

- **Countertop height, sink / range perimeter** (inset, left)
  - ☐ 34" above the floor (a compromise that works for both Rosemarie, 4'-2" seated, and Mark, 6'-4" standing)

KITCHEN — OVEN / MICROWAVE

- **Side door oven and microwave** permits up close access to contents without bending

- **Toe kick under base cabinets** – 9" tall by 6" deep.

- 5' diameter turning space in front of the oven and microwave.

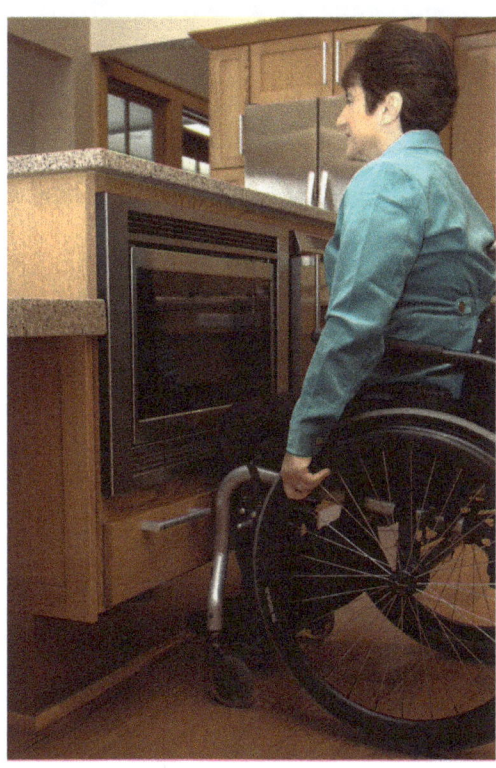

DIMENSIONS

# Universal Design Toolkit

KITCHEN — COOKING AREA

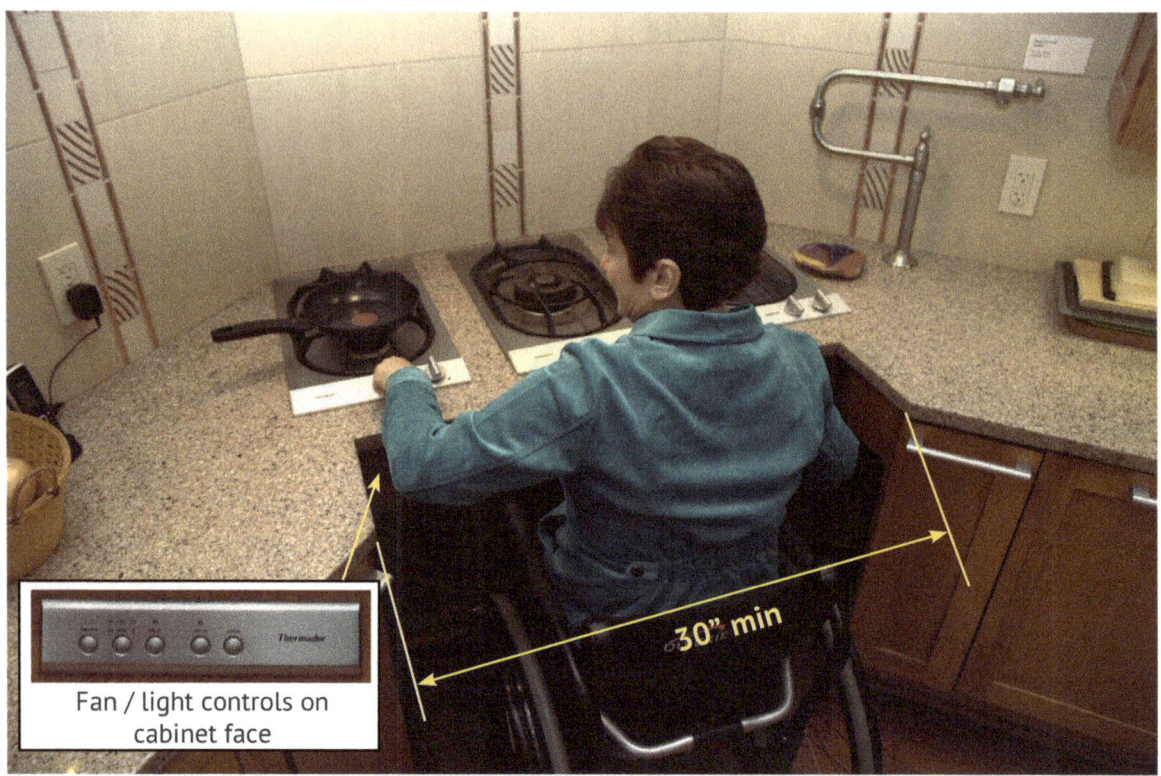

Fan / light controls on cabinet face

DIMENSIONS

- 30" wide access in front of the cooktop.

- 32" - 34" max height from the floor to the countertop.

- 27" minimum vertical knee space from floor to bottom of cabinet front. 29" high or greater is preferred to allow clearance for wheelchair armrests.

- Depth of knee space is 19".

- Front mounted controls for cooking units.

- Cabinet panel mounted (at Rosemarie's waist height) range hood controls.

Universal Design Toolkit

KITCHEN — SINK AREA

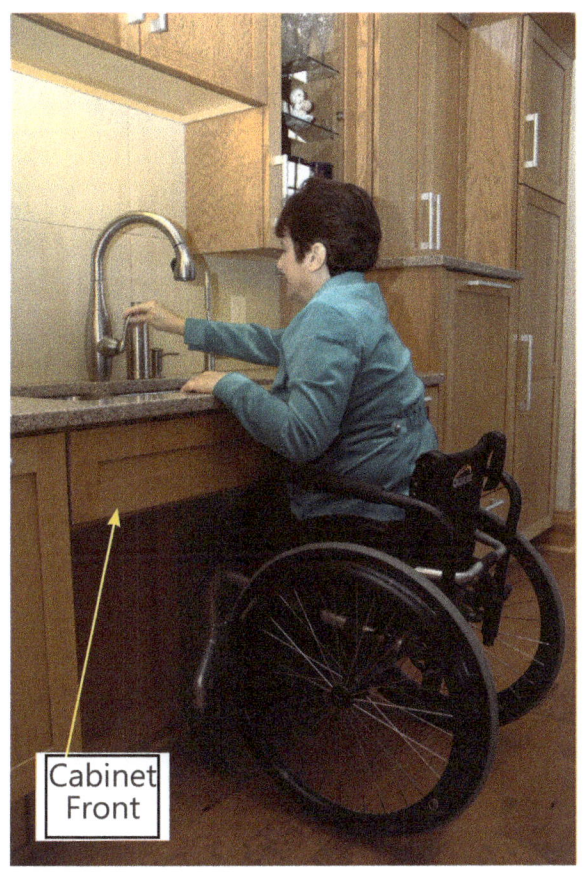

- **Kitchen sink depth installed over a knee space –** 6.5" with the drain towards the back.

- 32" - 34" max height from the floor to the countertop.

- 27" minimum vertical knee space from floor to **bottom** of cabinet front. 29" high or greater is preferred to allow clearance for wheelchair armrests.

- Depth of knee space is 10". The greater the depth, the better.

DIMENSIONS

 **Universal Design Toolkit**

KITCHEN — SINK AREA

- 15" wide minimum countertop space on one side of sink and 24" wide on other side.
- 36" wide x 48" deep approach in front of the sink (double bowl). The 36" width is the size of standard sink base cabinet.

DIMENSIONS

6. PROFESSIONALS: QUESTIONS TO ASK YOUR CLIENTS ABOUT THEIR CURRENT AND FUTURE NEEDS

1. Who will be living in the house with you? (parents, children, grandparents or grandchildren)

2. Does someone in your home have special needs due to physical, sensory and/or medical impairments and will need selected features in the home to accommodate them?

3. What health limitations do you or others you live with have that may impact the ease of living in your home?

4. Do you or anyone you live with have difficulty entering or exiting your home, moving from room to room, or using the kitchen or bathroom?

5. Are some activities more difficult now than they were in the past?

6. Do you have health conditions that may impact your ability to use certain spaces or rooms in your home?

7. What else about your health and prognosis should I know to do a good job on this project?

8. Is it important to you to have a full bathroom and bedroom on the first floor?

 Universal Design Toolkit

9. Do you have family members come to visit? Stay overnight? Do any have a disability?

10. How long do you want to live here? Do you plan to live in your home through retirement?

11. Have you engaged a design or building professional who is knowledgeable in adapting your living space to your lifestyle?

12. Will it be cost effective to remodel the home with universal design features to make it accessible, adaptable, safe and visitable?

13. Did you know that many home improvements for disabilities are tax deductible?

14. If something happens (i.e. a fall, broken bones, stroke, or dementia), can you and/or others still live in the home?

15. Is there a military veteran living in this home that may be able to receive a grant from the U.S. Department of Veterans Affairs to build a new home or fund home modifications?

16. Is there a person with a disability living in this home, who would like to be employed, and would be eligible to receive funding for home modifications from the state bureau of vocational rehabilitation?

Mims Mobley, David Good, and Mark Leder

SOURCES OF FUNDING TO REPAIR, MODIFY, REMODEL OR BUILD A NEW UNIVERSAL DESIGN HOME

People can find funding for their remodeling or new build projects through volunteer services, government assistance, direct funding, loans, as well as tax credits, deductions, and abatements.

Depending where you live, many states, counties, and cities have tax incentives and abatements to make home improvements and build accessible housing. Check with your local authorities to see if these are in place. Your community leaders can tell you if you qualify for city or state property tax credits or abatements as a result of your home modifications.

If you are disabled and purchase equipment for the home such as a porch lift or elevator, or modify the home by adding a ramp or widening the doors for access, the Internal Revenue Service does have tax deductions for these home improvements that are related to your disability. For information about federal tax deductions for your home improvements, contact the Internal Revenue Service and your tax accountant.

Private funds could be available by borrowing against home equity or taking out a second mortgage. For seniors, long-term care insurance is a great resource. Many long-term care policies have money that can be used for modifying a home for safety. Seniors also can use reverse mortgages to acquire funds for home modifications.

 Universal Design Toolkit

If you are a U.S. veteran there are many resources from the United States Department of Veterans Affairs. Take a look at the information listed below for phone numbers and website links.

Many federal, state, and local agencies have set aside public funds for accessible home modification. See these agencies below.

In addition there are corporate, private, and charitable organizations that provide volunteer services to help with the construction and donations of products to homeowners who qualify for this assistance. See the resources listed below and find out if you are eligible.

Religious and community groups provide volunteer services and funding to projects in their community. Contact service organizations like the Rotary Club, Lions Clubs International, and Kiwanis Club in your local community for funding and services.

Ask your healthcare provider for information on Medicare and Medicaid funding. Medical equipment or home modifications may be covered by insurance when prescribed by a doctor.

Universal Design Toolkit

If the remodeling is for a senior citizen, check with local, state, and national associations for information about special programs. These are often through Departments of Aging or the Area Agency on Aging. They can provide referrals or contractors to perform modification services for eligible seniors at no cost or at a low cost.

For people with disabilities who are planning to seek employment there are many avenues to explore including your State Department of Vocational Rehabilitation Agency. This department is funded with federal and state dollars. Funding can be used for home modifications for accessibility.

Independent Living Centers are located nationwide. People at the center should be aware of sources of funding, grant programs and contractors who can modify home to increase accessibility.

If your disability is a result of a progressive illness you may be eligible for assistance from a national association whose mission is to support the lives of people with this affliction. Some associations provide guides on home modifications that includes information about resources that can help people pay for home modifications. Examples include: United Spinal Association, American Cancer Society, National Multiple Sclerosis Society, National Muscular Dystrophy Association, National United Cerebral Palsy Association, National Parkinson Foundation, Alzheimer's Association.

For those in rural communities, the United States Department of Agriculture offers loans to low and moderate income households. See more details below.

Funding a home modification for a person with a financial need can be acquired through fundraising in the community, as well as online through crowdfunding websites. Establish a way to accept donations, contributions, and gifts, either at a bank, credit union, or a website like PayPal. Then, spread the word about the person's or family's need. Start with their own networks of relatives, co-workers, neighbors, and other acquaintances. People are more likely to give if they have some

Universal Design Toolkit

form of relationship with the people in need. Write a letter and a press release to the local radio, TV and news media and ask them to share this information with their audiences. Use social media sites, ask your friends to support then share your request for help with their own networks.

Here are resources to help find funding to modify or build a home for accessibility needs.

THESE SOURCES OF FUNDING ARE FOR UNITED STATES DISABLED VETERANS

United States Department of Veterans Affairs
Makes grants available to service members and veterans with certain permanent and total service-connected disabilities to help them buy or build an adapted home, or modify an existing home to accommodate a disability. The three grant programs are the Specially Adapted Housing grant, the Special Housing Adaptation grant, and the Home Improvement and Structural Alteration grant. You can apply online or call VA toll free at 1-800-827-1000 to have a claim form mailed to you.

http://www.benefits.va.gov/homeloans/adaptedhousing.asp
http://www.rehab.va.gov/PROSTHETICS/psas/HISA2.asp

Mark Mix

 Universal Design Toolkit

Foundations and nonprofit organizations also provide grants to disabled veterans.

Adaptive Homes
Provide transitional housing and home ownership to disabled veterans and their families. They fund home modifications and remodeling projects. Technology is provided for in-home health care services. They only operate in Ohio.

http://www.adaptivehomescdc.org

Building Homes for Heroes, Inc
This is a national non-profit, non-partisan 501(c)(3) organization founded in 2006 that builds or modifies homes, and gifts them, mortgage-free, to injured veterans who served in the wars in Iraq or Afghanistan.

http://buildinghomesforheroes.org

Gary Sinise Foundation
Helps wounded heroes increase their mobility and reclaim their self-reliance by building them specially adapted homes throughout the country.

https://www.garysinisefoundation.org/programs/rise

Home Depot Foundation
The Veteran Housing Grants Program awards grants to 501(c)3 nonprofit organizations for the development and repair of veterans housing. Funding is not provided to individuals. Many one-off single family home repair requests are a better fit for their Team Depot or Community Impact Grant programs. Veteran Housing Grants are best suited to fund single family home repairs when they are a part of a permanent program managed by the nonprofit partner.

https://corporate.homedepot.com/grants/veteran-housing-grants

 Universal Design Toolkit

Homes for Our Troops
Builds new mortgage-free, specially adapted homes nationwide for severely injured Veterans Post-9/11, to enable them to rebuild their lives. Most of these Veterans have sustained injuries including multiple limb amputations, partial or full paralysis, and/or severe traumatic brain injury.

http://www.hfotusa.org/

Jared Allen's Homes for Wounded Warriors
This foundation's mission is to provide financial assistance and support to our injured United States military veterans by building and remodeling handicap accessible homes to suit their individual needs one wounded warrior at a time.

https://www.homesforwoundedwarriors.com

Purple Heart Homes
Work with disabled veterans who were injured during their service to fund home repairs, remodeling and home modifications. They raise the funds for all approved and vetted projects through donations of money, labor and materials. They only operate in states where they have chapters throughout the country. They also have a program to assist in locating and assisting with financing a home.

https://www.purplehearthomesusa.org/

U.S. Army Wounded Warrior Program (AW2)
This program is a part of the Warrior Care and Transition Program. AW2 provides support to the Army's most severely wounded, ill and injured soldiers throughout their recovery, whether they are transitioning back to duty or into civilian life. This program supports these soldiers, veterans, their families and caregivers with the recovery and reintegration process to reach a state of self-sufficiency.

http://www.wtc.army.mil/wct/aw2_overview.html

Universal Design Toolkit

Wounded Warrior Project
Serves veterans and service members who incurred a physical or mental injury, illness, or wound, co-incident to their military service on or after September 11, 2001 and their families.

http://www.woundedwarriorproject.org/

THESE SOURCES OF FUNDING ARE FOR THE GENERAL PUBLIC

Access Loans through the Digital Federal Credit Union
These loans are for any product, device, or building modification designed to assist someone with a disability. The borrower need not be the beneficiary of the purchase. Accessible building modifications qualify such as: bathroom accessibility, kitchen modifications, widening doorways for wheelchairs, lowering countertops, changing cabinets, modifying sinks and faucets, installing ramps, elevators, stair climbing devices, installing ceiling lifts. Loans for those who qualify are from $1,500 to $25,000 and with terms up to 72 months.

https://www.dcu.org/loans/access.html

 Universal Design Toolkit

Aging and Disability Resource Center
Your local Aging and Disability Resource Center may be able to refer you to an organization or company that provides home modifications services. They offer information on long-term supports and services for older adults and people with disabilities.

http://www.adrc-tae.acl.gov/tiki-index.php?page=ADRCLocator

American Occupational Therapy Association Inc.
The American Occupational Therapy Association Inc. has information on what home modifications may be useful as well as how to seek funding for these improvements.

http://www.aota.org

American Parkinson Disease Association
This association has a nationwide network of chapters to help ease the burden of those with Parkinson's disease. Contact your local chapter to explore assistance options.

http://www.apdaparkinson.org

Benevolent and Protective Order of Elks
Elk Lodges are located throughout the USA, so contact your local chapter. Veterans as well as non-veterans can find out what kind of assistance they may be eligible to receive for home modifications.

http://www.elks.org/

Department of Vocational Rehabilitation Agency
For people with disabilities who would like to return to employment, contact your state vocational rehabilitation agency. Funding is available to make home modifications.

https://www.disability.gov/resource/vocational-rehabilitation-state-offices/

 Universal Design Toolkit

Easter Seals
Your local Easter Seals chapter www.easterseals.com can provide you with information about possible financing options to pay for modifications to make your home accessible. A free downloadable brochure that has tips on how to adapt your home to accommodate a person with a disability, "Easy Access Housing for Easier Living," was developed by Easter Seals and is distributed by the Century 21 System.

> http://www.easterseals.com/shared-components/document-library/easy_access_housing.pdf

Federal Assistance Program Information
Resources on government financial help in finding loans and grants to modify a home.

> https://www.usa.gov/repairing-home

Friends of Man
Helps people of all ages with a large variety of needs including ramps and home modifications. Referring professionals (health care and social workers, clergy, counselors, etc.) must submit applications on behalf of people in need of assistance.

> http://www.friendsofman.org

Habitat for Humanity
A nonprofit, Christian housing ministry. They build, renovate and repair houses all over the world using volunteer labor and donations. Habitat homeowners purchase their houses through affordable monthly mortgage payments. Families in need of decent, affordable shelter can apply to their programs.

> http://www.habitat.org/

 Universal Design Toolkit

HelpHopeLive
For people with spinal cord injuries, brain injuries and catastrophic injuries, start your own tax-exempt fundraising campaign through HelpHopeLive.

https://helphopelive.org

Internal Revenue Service
This Tax Benefits and Credits publication presents basic information about existing tax credits and benefits that may be available to qualifying taxpayers with disabilities, parents of children with disabilities, and businesses or other entities wishing to accommodate persons with disabilities.

https://www.irs.gov/pub/irs-pdf/p3966.pdf

Joseph Groh Foundation
Financially assists those with a connection to the construction trades industry (plumbing, HVAC, electrical, roofing etc.) who are living with a life-altering injury or illness. Assistance provided is designed to pay for the provision of material (i.e. durable medical equipment, etc.,) or services rendered (i.e. construction of ramps to the home, widening of doorways, reconstruction of bathrooms for wheelchair access, etc.)

http://josephgrohfoundation.org

 Universal Design Toolkit

Lions Clubs International
This is the world's largest service club organization. Contact your local chapter to see if you are eligible to receive assistance for home modifications.

> http://www.lionsclubs.org

Local Builder or Remodeler
According to Eldercare.gov, many minor home modifications and repairs cost between $150 and $2,000. Some home remodeling contractors offer reduced rates and charge sliding-scale fees based on a person's income and ability to pay. Contact a local builder or remodeler who may donate services and assist in contacting manufactures, distributors and suppliers to donate materials.

Medicaid: Home and Community Based Service Waivers
Home and community-based services provide opportunities for Medicaid beneficiaries to receive services in their own home or community. These programs serve a variety of targeted populations groups, such as people with mental illnesses, intellectual or developmental disabilities, and/or physical disabilities.

> https://www.medicaid.gov/Medicaid-CHIP-Program-Information/By-Topics/Long-Term-Services-and-Supports/Home-and-Community-Based-Services/Home-and-Community-Based-Services.html

In many states these waivers pay for home modifications to increase an individual's ability to live independently. Each state has different waivers with different eligibility requirements and benefits. A complete list of Medicaid programs that help with home modifications is available here.

> https://www.payingforseniorcare.com/home-modifications/medicaid-waivers.html

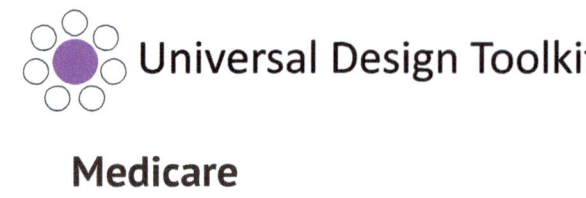 Universal Design Toolkit

Medicare
Medicare typically does not pay for the cost of home modifications; however, there are some exceptions. Medicare may pay for assistive technology devices that are part of the modification process provided they are required for medical reasons and prescribed by a doctor. One might also receive assistance from Medicare in determining what home modifications are medically required. Medicare Part B will pay for an occupational therapist to evaluate a home and determine what changes are required. In some rare instances, Medicare will pay for bathroom modifications and walk-in tubs or stair lifts.

https://www.payingforseniorcare.com/financial-assistance/walk-in-bathtubs-medicare.html

National Association of Area Agencies on Aging
Contact your local Area Agency on Aging for services. Some have home modification programs or can refer you to other organizations that can help pay for home repairs and modifications for senior citizens. They can often refer you to local contractors to do home modifications at a low cost.

http://www.n4a.org/

National Council for Independent Living
Contact your local Center for Independent Living and Statewide Independent Living Council who may be able to make some suggestions about how to pay for home modifications such as adding a wheelchair ramp or widening the doorway to your bathroom. They also provide advocacy and support services for people with disabilities, including assistance with housing, health care and independent living skills.

http://www.ncil.org/

 Universal Design Toolkit

National Council of State Housing Agencies
Contact your State Housing Finance Agency. Some state housing finance agencies have loan programs that help people with disabilities or who have a family member living in the household with disabilities, who are buying a home that needs accessibility modifications. Many states have home modification programs that are part of their state Assistive Technology programs. These programs provide low-interest loans to buy assistive technology or to help pay for home modifications and adaptations to make your home safe and accessible.

> https://www.ncsha.org/housing-help

National Resource Center on Supportive Housing and Home Modification
Promotes aging in place for seniors and people who are aging with a disability. The Center gives families and individuals the knowledge they need to plan for their housing, health and supportive service needs. Check your state's listings for agencies and organizations near you that can help with home modifications.

> http://gero.usc.edu/nrcshhm/index.htm

North Dakota Housing Finance Agency
For people with disabilities having low-incomes who live in North Dakota, the North Dakota Housing Finance Agency, under the Rehab Accessibility Program (RAP) helps fund accessibility improvements. Eligible improvements include the installation of wheelchair ramps, door levers, walk-in/roll-in showers or grab bars, and widening of doorways. The funds can be used to upgrade either single- or multi-family housing units. A maximum of $4,000 may be awarded with a limit of one grant per property in a fiscal year. Matching funds of at least 25 percent of the total project cost are required. For an application or more information on RAP:

> https://www.ndhfa.org/Rehab/RAP.html contact NDHFA at (800) 292-8621 or hfainfo@nd.gov

 Universal Design Toolkit

People Working Cooperatively, Inc.
For people living in Ohio, Kentucky and Indiana who have a low income, are elderly, or disabled, contact People Working Cooperatively, Inc. They provide residents with critical home repairs, energy conservation and weatherization, mobility modifications, and maintenance services.

http://www.pwchomerepairs.org

Rebuilding Together
A nonprofit organization that provides home repair and modification services for low-income families, people with disabilities, seniors and veterans and military families. Also helps families whose homes have been damaged by natural disasters. Contact your local affiliate for more information.

http://www.togetherwetransform.org/

Spinal Cord Opportunities for Rehabilitation Endowment
SCORE aims to assist young people who have been injured while participating in sporting events or athletic recreation. SCORE endeavors to improve the quality of life for people with a spinal cord injury, assisting with the substantial out-of-pocket costs associated with obtaining the best medical care, home modification, and transportation.

http://www.scorefund.org

Sunshine On A Ranny Day
A 501(c)(3) non-profit serving people within a 60 mile radius of Atlanta, GA, that renovate homes for children with special needs aged 3-19, at no cost to the family.

http://www.sunshineonaranneyday.com/

 Universal Design Toolkit

Travis Roy Foundation

Grants are awarded to spinal cord injury survivors with paraplegia and quadriplegia. Paralysis must be due to a spinal cord injury that was caused by an accident, separate from complications caused at birth. Eligible items for home modifications include: bath, ramp, and lift installations, bed/mattress, and shower chairs.

https://www.travisroyfoundation.org/sci/grants/application/

United States Department of Agriculture
Single Family Housing Repair Loans and Grants Program

Provides grants and loans to very low-income homeowners to repair, improve or modernize their homes and grants to elderly very low-income homeowners to remove health and safety hazards. Contact your USDA state office for more information about this program.

http://www.rd.usda.gov/programs-services/single-family-housing-repair-loans-grants

United States Department of Agriculture
Single Family Housing Direct Home Loan Program

Aassists low- and very-low-income applicants obtain decent, safe and sanitary housing in eligible rural areas by providing payment assistance to increase an applicant's repayment ability. Payment assistance is a type of subsidy that reduces the mortgage payment for a short time. The amount of assistance is determined by the adjusted family income.

http://www.rd.usda.gov/programs-services/single-family-housing-direct-home-loans

 Universal Design Toolkit

United States Department of Agriculture
Single Family Housing Guaranteed Loan Program

Assists approved lenders in providing low- and moderate-income households the opportunity to own adequate, modest, decent, safe and sanitary dwellings as their primary residence in eligible rural areas. Eligible applicants may build, rehabilitate, improve or relocate a dwelling in an eligible rural area.

http://www.rd.usda.gov/programs-services/single-family-housing-guaranteed-loan-program

United States Department of Housing and Urban Development
HOME Investment Partnerships Program

Provides formula grants to States and localities that communities use - often in partnership with local nonprofit groups - to fund a wide range of activities including building, buying, and/or rehabilitating affordable housing for rent or homeownership or

providing direct rental assistance to low-income people. HOME is the largest Federal block grant to state and local governments designed exclusively to create affordable housing for low-income households. The U.S. Department of Housing and Development (HUD) does not provide HOME assistance directly to individuals or organizations. If you are interested in participating in this program, you need to contact your local or state government to find out how the program operates in your area. Participation requirements may differ from one grantee to another. Find out who administers the HOME Program in your area or contact the HUD field office that serves your area. The local government administers the program and determines which local projects receive funding.

http://portal.hud.gov/hudportal/HUD?src=/program_offices/comm_planning/affordablehousing/programs/home/

United States Department of Housing and Urban Development Property Improvement Loan Insurance

A loan program to finance the light or moderate rehabilitation of properties.

http://portal.hud.gov/hudportal/HUD?src=/program_offices/housing/sfh/title/title-i

Search for crowdfunding websites for individuals on the Internet.

Crowdfunding refers to the practice of eliciting donations from a group to raise money towards a single goal. Individuals can create their own fundraising campaigns on crowdfunding platform websites to raise money for home modifications. Individuals can use their social media influence and emails to attract donors. Donations are made online and are collected by the crowdfunding sites who then deliver payment to the individual.

 Universal Design Toolkit

Here are some examples of crowdfunding websites for individuals.

https://www.crowdrise.com/

http://www.depositagift.com

http://fundly.com

https://fundrazr.com

http://www.giveforward.com

https://www.gofundme.com

https://gogetfunding.com

https://www.plumfund.com

https://rally.org

https://www.youcaring.com

Search for foundation grants for individuals at your local library.

Ask the reference librarian to locate directories online and in print. Most of the foundations do not give grants to individuals, but rather they fund non-profit associations. Most forms of assistance for individuals with disabilities will come from charitable organizations or government assistance programs, rather than grants from foundations.

Here are some online directories and sources of information.

- Foundation Center
  http://foundationcenter.org
- Foundation Directory Online
  https://fconline.foundationcenter.org/
- Foundation Grants to Individuals Online
  http://gtionline.foundationcenter.org/
- Grants for Individuals: The Disabled
  http://staff.lib.msu.edu/harris23/grants/3disable.htm

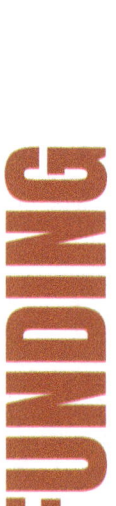

 Universal Design Toolkit

- Grantspace
  http://grantspace.org
- Grant Watch
  http://www.grantwatch.com

Search the Internet
Look for housing grants, housing grants for people with disabilities, and housing grants for veterans.

8 HOW TO FIND A PROFESSIONAL WHO IS KNOWLEDGEABLE ABOUT UNIVERSAL DESIGN

(Architect, Home Designer, Builder, Remodeler, Interior Designer, Lighting Designer, Occupational Therapist, Landscape Designer and Realtor)

As you approach a home remodeling or new build project and want to include universal design features, it is important that you select people who are experienced and knowledgeable to help with the home design and construction. There are many professional organizations offering certification for their members. See the list below. This makes the selection process a little easier. Many organizations post directories of their members on their websites so that you can search for one of their members who lives in your community. If there is not a directory of their members, make a call to the organization to locate a member. It is highly advised that you select people who live close to your project. It is important that you review the person's credentials but it is more important that you interview the candidate in person and get at least three references of people who have hired them in the recent past. Contact these references and see what type of work this person did and how satisfied the reference person was with the work performed.

The Federal Trade Commission website includes many tips to find and hire a contractor as well as a way to report contractors when there are problems. https://www.consumer.ftc.gov/articles/0242-hiring-contractor

Universal Design Toolkit

When building or remodeling there is much involved in getting the design right from the beginning. You have an option to work with an architect or home designer. If the builder or remodeler includes the design services in their proposal, then make sure that person has had experience with designing homes with universal design features and products.

It is also a benefit that the builder or remodeler has taken additional course work in the field of universal design or aging in place. In addition, find out how much experience the builder or remodeler has in universal design home construction.

Hiring an interior designer is very beneficial in creating the floor plan as well as selecting finishes, colors, fabric, art, ornamentation, door and window hardware, lighting fixtures, appliances, furniture placement and selection, plumbing fixtures, and other elements of the interior of the home. Interior design also involves considerations that affect comfort, function and safety. Among these are lighting, acoustics, space planning, organization and storage, scale, fire safety, compliance with local building codes, and accommodation of special needs for a person with a disability.

Universal Design Toolkit

Illumination is important in a home and landscape. A lighting designer on your design team can locate lighting fixtures that will be built into your home and landscape as well as specify the fixtures, equipment, bulbs, lighting controls, and sensors. More lighting is needed as our eyes age. Lighting in key areas of the home such as entries and stairways can prevent falls. Lighting creates visibility, color, and creates a mood. The quality and quantity of light from windows, doors, skylights and artificial sources all contribute to the lighting in a home.

For a person with a disability who will be living in the home, an occupational therapist is another specialist to get involved in the project. An occupational therapist has the educational background and experience to know how a person with a disability can be supported by their physical environment as well as through supports such as medical equipment and mobility aids.

A landscape architect or landscape designer should also be a part of your design team. The landscape views from inside the home should be a part of the discussion early in the design process. Equally important is discussion about how to enter the landscape from the home. Step free entrances are critically important so people who use wheelchairs and walkers have full access. The property elevations will need to be reviewed to accommodate access in the landscape. Smooth level patio and porch surfaces will need to be selected for ease in rolling across in a wheelchair.

Assemble all members of the design team and have them meet with you to discuss your needs. It is better to get the team involved early in the planning process rather than later. Early planning is very important. Costly mistakes in the design process show up during construction.

If you are 50+ and in the market to buy a new or existing home, or sell your current home, you may decide to work with a Realtor. The National Association of Realtors has a certification program in place, Senior Real Estate Specialists, for real estate professionals who want to have a focus on serving the 50+ market.

 Universal Design Toolkit

Here are some resources to help in your search to find professionals to join your team.

HOME TRADE ASSOCIATIONS

National Association of Home Builders
Certified Aging-in-Place Specialist

http://www.nahb.org/en/learn/designations/certified-aging-in-place-specialist.aspx

National Association of REALTORS®
Seniors Real Estate Specialist® - certification

http://www.seniorsrealestate.com/Find-SRES/find

National Association of the Remodeling Industry
Universal Design Certified Professional

http://www.nari.org/industry/development/certification/universal-design-certified-professional-udcp/

National Kitchen and Bath Association
http://www.nkba.org

Universal Design Toolkit

CROSS-DISCIPLINE CERTIFICATION PROGRAMS

Accessible Home Improvement of America
Certified Environmental Access Consultant

http://www.accesshomeamerica.com/ceac.asp

Living in Place Institute
Certified Living in Place Professional

http://livinginplaceinstitute.org/

HOME DESIGN TRADE ASSOCIATIONS

American Institute of Architects
http://www.aia.org/

American Institute of Building Design
http://www.aibd.org/

Society of American Registered Architects
http://www.sara-national.org

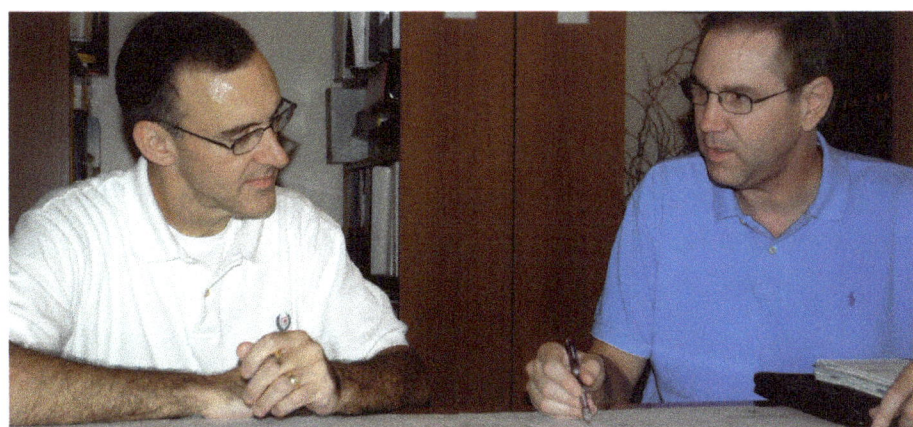
UDLL architect Patrick Manley and Mark Leder

 Universal Design Toolkit

INTERIOR DESIGN TRADE ASSOCIATIONS

American Society of Interior Designers
www.asid.org

Designer Society of America
http://www.dsasociety.org

Interior Design Society
http://www.interiordesignsociety.org

International Interior Design Association
www.iida.org

LANDSCAPE DESIGN TRADE ASSOCIATIONS

American Society of Landscape Architects
https://www.asla.org/

Association of Professional Landscape Designers
https://www.apld.org

International Federation of Landscape Architects
http://iflaonline.org

LIGHTING DESIGN TRADE ASSOCIATIONS

American Lighting Association
http://www.americanlightingassoc.com

Certified Lighting Designer
http://www.cld.global/

Illuminating Engineering Society
http://www.ies.org

International Association of Lighting Designers
https://www.iald.org/

National Lighting Bureau
http://www.nlb.org/

OCCUPATIONAL THERAPY TRADE ASSOCIATION

American Occupational Therapy Association
Specialty Certification in Environmental Modification

http://www.aota.org/Education-Careers/Advance-Career/Board-Specialty-Certifications/SpecialtyCert.aspx

CONSUMERS: QUESTIONS TO ASK WHEN SELECTING A DESIGNER AND BUILDER/ REMODELER

1. Are you certified as an Aging in Place Specialist (CAPS) from the National Association of Home Builders?

2. Have you taken the Universal Design/Build class from the National Association of Home Builders?

3. Are you certified as a Universal Design Certified Professional (UDCP) through the National Association of the Remodeling Industry?

4. What certifications do you have that are relevant to universal design?

5. What universal design courses or conferences have you attended?

6. How many homes, including your own, have you built with universal design features?

7. How long have you been building homes with universal design features?

8. Who would design my future kitchen and bathrooms?

Universal Design Toolkit

9. Do you have ranch-style as well as two-story floor plans that include universal design features?

10. When I select a floor plan from your inventory, if changes are needed, who makes them?

11. When I select a floor plan, must it be one that you provide? If not, where do I look for a universal design floor plan?

12. Can you give me three recent referrals for homes you have built with universal design features?

13. Can you build my home without steps from the garage into the home?

14. How and where will you reinforce the walls in the bathrooms for the installation of grab bars?

15. How will you design my home so I can install an elevator at a future time?

16. How will you design the cabinets in the kitchen and bathroom so I will have knee space under the sinks and cooktop?

17. Will you come to my current home to see how it is set up, watch how I get around, and look for any trouble spots? Will you help me identify how to correct and improve my independence and safety in my home for now and for the future?

18. Will you have a floor plan with your price quote so I can see what is being proposed?

 **Universal Design Toolkit**

19. Will you have renderings or images of the new proposed home?

20. Will you have a detailed proposal, a job schedule with a timeline, and a payment schedule tied to specific milestones?

21. What licenses and insurance do you have?

22. Will you obtain the building permits? If not you, who will?

Manley Architecture Group

10 HOW TO FIND HOUSE PLANS, FLOOR PLANS AND ROOM DESIGNS FOR UNIVERSAL DESIGN HOMES

There are many resources and people to help create house plans including universal design consultants, architects, home designers, builders, remodelers, and interior designers. Sample house plans can be purchased to serve as a starting point. There are many books and magazines in the fields of architecture, home building and interior design that include house plans. Check out your local library and the Internet. An architect or home designer can create a custom house plan based on criteria desired. The Internet has several sites with house plans. Examples are:

http://www.builderhouseplans.com/

http://www.dreamhomesource.com/

http://www.eplans.com/

https://www.floorplans.com

http://www.homeplans.com/

https://www.houseplans.com/

These plans may include universal design features; however a more comprehensive search will be needed to find plans that specifically include universal design features. An architect who is knowledgeable about universal design can work with a client to make sure the house plan is adjusted to include universal design features.

 Universal Design Toolkit

On the Internet there are extensive photos of homes and rooms at www.pinterest.com and www.houzz.com Do a search on "universal design" at these sites to help with your research. You will see photos of products and illustrations in addition to completed rooms in homes.

There are many television shows featuring home design. Many are on the HGTV channel. www.hgtv.com By watching these shows you will start to know what architectural styles and interior design ideas you are attracted to. Occasionally these shows feature universal design homes.

Builders can supply floor plans of their model homes and may be knowledgeable about universal design features that can be included. As you tour model homes, ask what other house plans the builders have in their inventory for your consideration.

A ranch-style home is one option; however, a two story home that can accommodate the installation of an elevator in the future will also be an option to consider. Closets can be stacked, one on each floor that are sized appropriately for the future installation of an elevator.

When working with an architect or home designer for a custom home design, share photos of homes you have seen as well as photos in books, magazines and on the Internet. This will convey the architectural style that you prefer for the exterior and interior of the home.

Consider the sizes of each of the rooms in your existing home and decide if the new home size should be similar, larger, or smaller. The total home square footage is a prime measurement due to the construction cost, as well as how it will serve the people who will live there now and in the future. Design from the inside to the outside. It is important that you have the rooms properly sized and in the correct proximity to each other. Keep in mind your needs to facilitate ease of use, functionality, and maintaining privacy. Sketch out a basic floor plan to share each room's location and approximate size when you start a floor plan.

 Universal Design Toolkit

Books and Links to House Plans, Floor Plans and Room Designs

"**Accessible Home Design: Architectural Solutions for the Wheelchair User**" Second Edition, Thomas D. Davies and Carol Peredo Lopez, Paralyzed Veterans of America Distribution Center, 2006

"**AARP Guide to Revitalizing Your Home: Beautiful Living for the Second Half of Life**", Rosemary Bakker, Lark, 2010

"**Bathroom Options for Multifamily Housing in North Carolina**", The Center for Universal Design, North Carolina State University, 2005

https://www.ncsu.edu/www/ncsu/design/sod5/cud/pubs_p/docs/qap_tech_screen.pdf

"**Houses That Work for Life!**", Lisa Sandlin, Booksurge Publishing, 2009

"**Human Factors in the Built Environment**", Linda L. Nussbaumer, Fairchild Books, 2014

"**Inclusive Design: A Universal Need**", Linda L. Nussbaumer, Fairchild Books, 2012

"**Residential Design for Aging in Place**", Drew Lawlor and Michael A. Thomas, Wiley, 2008

"**Universal Design for the Home: Great-Looking, Great-Living Design for All Ages, Abilities, and Circumstances**", Wendy A. Jordan, Quarry Books, 2008

"**Universal Design Ideas for Style, Comfort & Safety**", RSMeans and Lexicon Consulting Inc., 2007

 Universal Design Toolkit

Architects Who Promote and Sell Their Universal Design House Plans

Rick Thompson, Architect 828-734-2553 rick@thompsonplans.com Lake Junaluska, North Carolina
https://www.thompsonplans.com/house-plans/universal-design-plans/

Interior designers Eric Moore and Anna Lyon with Rosemarie

11 ESTIMATED CONSTRUCTION AND PRODUCT COSTS FOR SELECTED UNIVERSAL DESIGN FEATURES

ENTRYS

Zero step entrance
$100-$600 based on the foundation used. Average $300. Bolingbrook IL passed an ordinance in 2002 requiring every new house to have one zero-step entrance. In 2014, the city Building Commissioner confirmed by letter that nearly 4,000 homes had already been constructed with zero step entrances over basements, at no added cost. On sites where the zero step entrance would be difficult due to the slope, there will be additional costs.

Average cost to retrofit a home to include a ramp
Range $1,600 - $3,200.

BATHROOMS

SHOWERS

Install a curbless modular shower
$2,000 - $4,500. An acrylic shower surround with a built-in bench costs no more than a plain stall.

 Universal Design Toolkit

Install a curbless custom tiled shower
$5,000 - $15,000. Installing a curbless shower costs about the same as installing a fully tiled shower with a curb. $200 - $300 in labor for modifying floor joists.

A built-in corner bench in a tiled shower
$150 to $250

A built –in folding shower seat
$150 to $500

A portable shower stool
$50 - $150

Hand-held shower head units
Are no more expensive than fixed shower heads. $50 - $100

Removing a tub and replacing it with a curbless shower
$8,000 - $10,000

GRAB BARS

Plywood for reinforcement
$250 for labor and materials for a 3' X 5' enclosure

Grab bar
$20 – $300 depending on the size and finish

Installation of grab bar
$50 – $125

TOILET
$0 - $50 (not including installation) additional cost for a toilet with a toilet seat that is 16"–18" high from the floor, compared to a 14" or 15" high toilet seat.

LEVER-STYLE PLUMBING FAUCET HANDLES
$0. At comparable prices of other plumbing faucet handles.

 Universal Design Toolkit

DOORS

Door width price differential
Cost added using a 36" door vs. a 30" door
- **Hollow core:** + $5.00
- **Solid core:** + $8.00
- **Solid poplar:** + $20.00

Replacing a Narrow Door
- New 36" wide door: $85 - $248
- New 34' of casing (3½" wide): $36 - $59
- Labor per door: $100 - $200
- Total: $221 - $507 per door including new framing, trim, door and labor

Swing away door hinge $18/pair

Lever-style door handles $0.
At comparable prices of knob-style door handles.

KITCHEN

Raised dishwasher
$0 - $200 depending if a drawer is installed under the dishwasher.

Cooktop and range controls on the front of the unit
$0. At comparable prices of units with the controls in the back.

 Universal Design Toolkit

ELECTRICAL

Electrical outlet box position on the wall
$0. 20" from the floor to the center of the electrical outlet box.

Light switch position on the wall
$0. 42" from the floor to the center of the light switch.

OTHER FEATURES

Elevator
$25,000 and up installed. An elevator would run between $25,000 and $35,000 furnished and installed (new construction) depending on options included such as: power gates, power doors, drive system, number of stops, and number of openings on the car. If the elevator were being installed in an existing home, construction costs would need to be added to the previous numbers.

Stair lift
$3,000 - $14,000 installed. A typical straight run chairlift would run about $3,600. A turning unit would be approximately $14,000 depending on the number of turns and the length of the stairs.

12 UNIVERSAL DESIGN FEATURES CHECKLIST BY ROOM AT THE UNIVERSAL DESIGN LIVING LABORATORY

The features listed here are all installed in the Universal Design Living Laboratory, the national demonstration home and garden in Columbus, OH. Awarded three certifications for universal design excellence, it is presently the top rated home for such attributes in North America.

Even though this demonstration home has an enhanced level of features and finishes, do not be discouraged, as universal design can be incorporated into any new home from production to luxury at very minimal cost. Even renovation projects that include UD features would benefit current and future homeowners.

Realize that a new or renovation project does not have to include all these features. Adapting even just a few of these features would be a step in the right direction.

How to use this report:

A great way to benefit from this report is to let it be your companion as you tour the home virtually. Our project partner Google photographed all the rooms in the home. This immersive experience will help you solidify your awareness of universal design features.

The virtual tour is located at http://www.udll.com/virtual-tour

Please reach out to us if you have other questions at the email address listed below.

 Universal Design Toolkit

The Entries

- Low thresholds at any door, no higher than ½"
- 36" wide doors with lever handles
- Lighting for safety and access
- Porch shielded from the weather
- High visibility house address numbers
- 5' x 5' level maneuvering space (turning circle) on both sides of door
- Stepless, level grade at the entrance
- Sloped garage floor to the house entry with low threshold
- Use sloping walks, earth berms, retaining walls, bridges, or porches instead of obtrusive front ramps
- Package shelf or bench outside the door
- Full-length sidelight(s) and door glass at entry door to see visitors

FEATURES

1/2" maximum threshold change between different finish floor surfaces

Universal Design Toolkit

The Kitchen

- Sufficient clear floor space for work/traffic flow; 5 foot turning radius
- Circulation routes 40" wide at a minimum at entryways to the kitchen
- No thresholds at any door
- 36" wide doors with lever handles
- Easy to roll on hard surface flooring
- Point of use storage
- Open/visible storage; flexible pantry storage
- Flexible base storage allowing for use as knee space
- Roll-out cart for storage
- Single lever faucets, mounted to the rear of a low profile sink
- Pot filler at cooktop

- Garbage disposer mounted in the rear of the sink allowing for knee space under the sink
- D-shaped handles rather than knobs on cabinets and drawers
- Counter tops at a variety of common heights: 30", 34", 35", and 40"
- Roll-out full extension shelves and drawers in lower cabinets

 Universal Design Toolkit

The Kitchen (continued)

- Toe kick area at the base of lower cabinets: 9-10" high by 6" deep
- Glass doors on upper cabinets
- Vertical (pantry style) cabinet with pull out shelving for most used items
- Waste and recycling container on pull-out drawer in lower cabinet
- Pull out spice racks
- Side hinged doors on oven and microwave at counter height or lower
- Dishwasher elevated 16" above the floor
- Front-mounted controls on cooktop with easy to read print
- Knee space under sink and cooktop
- Side by side refrigerator/freezer (prefer 24" deep) w/ full extension shelves

- Electrical wall outlets 18" above the floor
- Electrical outlets and controls within reach Ex. Garbage disposer, range hood ventilation
- Varied light sources (LED and halogen)
- Under cabinet LED tape lighting
- Adjustable lighting controls with dimmer switches
- Light switches should have rocker switch, and be located within easy reach of user, (not on the back wall!) 42-48" off the floor

Universal Design Toolkit

The Bathrooms

- 36" wide pocket doors as a space saving alternative
- Circulation routes 40" wide at a minimum, to get to the bathroom
- Sufficient clear floor space for functional passage
- 5' turning radius in key areas
- Point of use, easily accessed storage
- No threshold entries
- Toe kick area at the base of lower cabinets: 9-10" high by 6" deep
- Increased use of support rails and grab bars in the toileting, shower and tub areas that compliment the aesthetics
- Walls reinforced with ¾" plywood and wood blocking behind wallboards where grab bars will be installed
- Heat in the floor and a towel warmer
- Anti-scald fittings on tub and shower
- Non-slip flooring
- Controls for lighting and fixtures that are easy to operate
- Vanity mirror at height for a seated person
- Multiple-height vanities with knee space under the sink

The Bathrooms (continued)

- Channel shower drain
- Curbless shower
- Full length mirror
- Wall mounted shower chair
- Towel bars at various heights for access by people who sit and those who stand
- Hand-held shower spray on a sliding vertical bar, with 60" long hose
- Water controls within reach of person seated in the shower
- Tub deck extended 15" for easier entry
- Tub with non-slip bottom
- Tub with built in grab bars
- Comfort-height toilets with seats 17-18" above the floor
- Toilet centered 18" from a side wall so grab bars can be within easy reach
- Increased lighting from varied sources with adjustable controls
- Sufficient, well shielded lighting along either side of vanity mirror to eliminate shadows while grooming
- Moderate light level for wayfinding and orientation from bed to bathroom during the night
- Electrical outlets and controls within reach
- Lighted rocker switches, located within easy reach of user, (not on the back wall!) 42-48" off the floor
- Electrical wall outlets 18" above the floor

Universal Design Toolkit

The Wardrobe/Laundry

- Front-loading washer and dryer with front controls installed on a raised storage platform with drawers.
- Utility sink with knee space underneath
- Tall windows and a skylight provide natural lighting and ensure privacy
- Wall-mounted ironing board that adjusts in height for a person who is seated or standing
- Motion-activated lighting system
- Location of laundry appliances and clothing storage within same room increases efficiency
- Use of pocket doors to save space and allow for privacy
- Full length mirror
- Center island allows for accessible storage and a place to pack and unpack luggage and fold clothing
- Full extension drawers
- More than 50% of storage space is 54" or less from floor

FEATURES

 Universal Design Toolkit

The Bedrooms

- Light switches are illuminated rocker switches
- Electrical outlets are located at a minimum of 20" above the floor form the top of box
- Carbon monoxide detector in all bedrooms
- Ceiling fan
- The hardwood floor is wheelchair friendly.
- 36" wide door which allows for 32" clearance
- Pocket door to save space and have the ability to keep light out of the bedroom if someone is in the bathroom

- Sound reducing property of all drywall in this room to keep this room quiet and keep out the street noise
- 36" of clear space around the sides and foot of the king size bed
- The adjustable frame king size bed is 27" high with a memory foam mattress and a massage unit
- The sheets have pockets on each side. Convenient to store remote controls, tissues, glasses, medications and ear plugs
- Casement windows with locks that are reachable from a seated position

Universal Design Toolkit

The Landscape / Patio

- A level covered patio with a concrete floor having ample room for a dining table, chairs, and a barbeque grill.

- Permeable pavers are ADA-compliant so that people are less likely to slip and fall when walking on them. They have a surface that is easy to roll on in a wheelchair, resulting in less vibration to the wheelchair user.

- Raised garden beds that are accessible from a seated position.

- Plants are in large containers that are accessible from a seated position.

- A water hydrant is on the patio with light weight hoses attached.

- The retaining walls provide for seating and access to the planting bed.

- The fire pit is positioned with ample space for seating around it including space for large wheelchairs.

- The three foot wide paver pathway from the lower paver patio to the upper paver patio has a 1:20 slope making it easier for those using manual wheelchairs.

- Step free entrances, 36" wide doors, and low door thresholds at all access points from the home to the patio.

13 UNIVERSAL DESIGN CHECKLISTS, SAFETY CHECKLISTS, HOME ASSESSMENTS, AND CERTIFICATION PROGRAMS

UNIVERSAL DESIGN CHECKLISTS

Aging in Place: Universal Design Home Checklist
An extensive checklist created by the University of Arkansas, Cooperative Extension Service. Written by LaVona Traywick, Ph.D., MA, CFLE - Assistant Professor of Gerontology, 2007

http://www.universaldesignar.org/sites/default/files/uploads/UniversalDesignchecklist.pdf

Adapting a Home for Wheelchair Accessibility
The LIFE Center at the Rehabilitation Institute of Chicago created a listing of modifications, specifications and suggestions for each room in a home so that space is created for people who use wheelchairs.

https://lifecenter.ric.org/index.php?tray=content&cid=2246

AARP Home Fit Guide
A free booklet with universal design checklists and tips for livability, safety, maintenance, energy savings, and finding a contractor or occupational therapist.

http://assets.aarp.org/www.aarp.org_/articles/families/HousingOptions/200590_HomeFit_rev011108.pdf

CHECKLISTS

 Universal Design Toolkit

You can read the contents online at:

http://www.aarp.org/livable-communities/info-2014/aarp-home-fit-guide-aging-in-place.html

Creating Accessible Homes
A checklist of universal design features for the entire home as well as listings in the kitchen, bathroom, bedroom, stairs, laundry and entrances. Developed by Kansas State University Agricultural Experiment Station and Cooperative Extension Service

http://www.maraisdescygnes.k-state.edu/home-family-moneymanagement/energy-and-housing/energy-housing-information/creatingaccessiblehomes.pdf

Easy Access Housing for Easier Living
A free booklet developed by Easter Seals and distributed by the Century 21 System.

http://www.easterseals.com/shared-components/document-library/easy_access_housing.pdf

General Kitchen Design Tips: Universal Kitchen Checklist
Use these handy checklists for hints on creating a workable kitchen. Created by Mary Jo Peterson www.mjpdesign.com The following lists are intended to inspire ideas for incorporating universal access into kitchens.

http://www.loghome.com/kitchen-design-tips-2/

Gold, Silver and Bronze Universal Design Features in Houses
A collection of universal design features that are recommended for various rooms in a home. The Center for Universal Design, College of Design, North Carolina State University.

http://www.ncsu.edu/www/ncsu/design/sod5/cud/pubs_p/docs/GBS.pdf

Universal Design Toolkit

Home Adaptation Checklist
The Canadian Safety Council posted a room by room checklist to help people create homes that are safe and provide for independence.

https://canadasafetycouncil.org/home-safety/home-adaptation-checklist

Home Checklist
Northwest Universal Design Council in Seattle, WA created this checklist that was adapted with permission from a Practical Guide to Universal Home Design.

http://www.environmentsforall.org/home-checklist/

Maintaining Seniors' Independence Through Home Adaptations
The Canadian Safety Council published this booklet that is designed for seniors, but is usable by all. It identifies the types of difficulties people can experience in the home and describes adaptations to overcome these difficulties. This guide helps people assess their own unique circumstances including using stairs, moving around the house, doing laundry and answering the door.

http://www.cmhc-schl.gc.ca/odpub/pdf/61087.pdf?fr=1452708653491

My Child Without Limits
References a listing of home modification guidelines for children with cerebral palsy.

http://www.mychildwithoutlimits.org/plan/assistive-technology/home-modification/home-modification-guidelines/

 Universal Design Toolkit

New Home Universal Design Option Checklist
California Department of Housing and Community Development. A checklist created in 2007 of universal design features to guide builders and architects during the design and building process. California law, section 17959.6 of the Health and Safety Code, requires a builder of new for-sale residential units to provide buyers with a list of specific "universal design features" which make a home safer and easier to use for persons who are aging or frail, or who have certain temporary or permanent activity limitations or disabilities.

> http://www.hcd.ca.gov/codes/shl/ModelChecklistFinal1-10-07Version.pdf

Practical Guide to Universal Home Design
A free booklet for remodeling or building homes with universal design features. Includes checklists for each room. Produced by East Metro Seniors Agenda for Independent Living with support from the Minnesota Department of Human Services.

> http://www.environmentsforall.org/files/2015/10/practicalguide.pdf

Remodeling Today for a Better Tomorrow: Design Ideas for the Kitchen and Bathroom
A free booklet created by The Hartford Center for Mature Market Excellence, 2015.

> http://www.thehartford.com/sites/thehartford/files/remodeling-guide.pdf

Universal Design Toolkit

Universal Design & Green Home Survey Checklist
University of Iowa Clinical Law Programs, Leonard A. Sandler. April 2016. Includes checklists for the exterior and interior of a home looking at universal design as well as several green features. A comprehensive document to review features needed in each room in a home.

>http://law.uiowa.edu/universal-design-green-home-survey-checklist

Universal Design Checklists
AARP has a list of seven physical disabilities that can be addressed with universal design solutions including: using a wheelchair, limited reach, poor hand strength, poor balance, limited hearing, and vision impairment.

>http://www.aarp.org/home-garden/home-improvement/info-04-2005/home_special_needs_checklist.html

Universal Design Checklists
Shared Solutions America is a national non-profit organization and resource center for education, technology, and funding alternatives for seniors and people of all ages with disabilities. Includes checklists, articles and information on livable and universal design homes.

>http://livablehomes.org/safety-checklist

Universal Design in Housing
A free booklet that includes characteristics and benefits of universal design features. Prepared by the Center for Universal Design, North Carolina State University, College of Design

>http://www.ncsu.edu/www/ncsu/design/sod5/cud/pubs_p/docs/UDinHousing.pdf

Universal Design Toolkit

Cooking Center Design Tips: Universal Kitchen Design Checklist
Created by Mary Jo Peterson www.mjpdesign.com

http://www.loghome.com/cooking-range-oven/

Preparation Station Design Tips: Universal Kitchen Design Checklist
Created by Mary Jo Peterson www.mjpdesign.com

http://www.loghome.com/prep-station/

Sink/Clean-Up Center Design Tips: Universal Kitchen Design Checklist
Created by Mary Jo Peterson www.mjpdesign.com

http://www.loghome.com/sink-clean-up-center/

 Universal Design Toolkit

UNIVERSAL DESIGN CERTIFICATION PROGRAMS THAT INCLUDE UNIVERSAL DESIGN CHECKLISTS

Better Living Design

http://www.betterlivingdesign.org

The Better Living Design Institute™ will offer a BLD™ Certification for builders, remodelers and designers. This program is being developed in conjunction with leading trade organizations and will educate professionals on Better Living Design™ and the criteria associated with the "BLD Approved™" designation.

Lifelong Housing

http://rvcog.org/mn.asp?pg=SDS_Lifelong_Housing

Is only available in select areas in Oregon. The Rogue Valley Council of Government's Lifelong Housing Certification Project is a voluntary certification process for evaluating the accessibility and/or adaptability of homes.

Livable Design by Eskaton

http://www.livabledesign.com/

There are three levels of the Seal of Approval. To download the free guidebook containing universal design checklists:

> http://www.livabledesign.com/wp-content/uploads/2015/06/FINAL6.11.15Livable.Design.Program.Criteria.V8.pdf

ZeroStep

http://www.dakc.us/

Disability Advocates of Kent County, Michigan created this universal design certification program.

 **Universal Design Toolkit**

SAFETY CHECKLISTS

10 Safety Hazards to Watch Out for Around the House
An article by Rebecca Edwards that highlights the hazards in the kitchen, bathroom, fire, falling, poisoning, and choking hazards.

http://www.safewise.com/blog/10-safety-hazards-to-watch-out-for-around-the-house/

Accident Prevention: A Safe Home is No Accident
A free downloadable brochure to learn about how accidents can happen at home and how to prevent them. Developed by Easter Seals and distributed by the Century 21System.

http://www.easterseals.com/shared-components/document-library/a_safe_home_is_no_accident.pdf

A Housing Safety Checklist for Older People
North Carolina State University, North Carolina Cooperative Extension Service. A series of checklists for use in various rooms in a home to help make the home safer.

http://www.ces.ncsu.edu/depts/fcs/pdfs/FCS-461.pdf

Centers for Disease Control and Prevention - Children (Ages 4-11) - Safety in the Home & Community
A vast selection of topics to help avoid accidents with children including topics about home safety.

http://www.cdc.gov/parents/children/safety.html

CHECKLISTS

Universal Design Toolkit

Checklist for Environmental Safety – For People who are Blind or Visually Impaired

A listing from the American Foundation for the Blind to help spot areas to improve in the home regarding lighting, stairways, hallways, color contrast, eliminating hazards, and furniture placement.

> http://www.afb.org/info/low-vision/living-with-low-vision/a-checklist-for-environmental-safety/235

Checklist for Stairways

Tips from Jake Pauls, CPE to make stairways safe by learning about steps, handrails and how to make stairways visible.

> http://www.bldguse.com/Checklist_for_Stairways.html

Childproofing Experts

Important safety steps for each milestone in your child's life.

> http://www.childproofingexperts.com/

Childproofing Your Home

A checklist of items to keep out of reach of children to prevent harm, choking, and poisoning.

> https://www.healthychildren.org/English/safety-prevention/at-home/Pages/Childproofing-Your-Home.aspx

Creating a Comfortable Environment for People with Low Vision

The American Foundation for the Blind provides suggestions for environmental adaptations or modifications that enhance functioning for people with low vision.

> http://www.afb.org/info/low-vision/living-with-low-vision/creating-a-comfortable-environment-for-people-with-low-vision/235

# Universal Design Toolkit

Creating an Optimum Home Environment for Children with Autism Spectrum Disorders
An article describing home modifications that would create a comfortable and safe environment for children with autism spectrum disorders.

http://www.autism-programs.com/articles-on-autism/optimum-home-environment-for-children-with-autism.htm

Home Safety for People with Disabilities
Information about fire sprinklers and alarms in the event of a fire, as well as information on how to escape a home should there be a fire.

http://www.nfpa.org/disabilities

Home Safety for People with Disabilities
Article by Tom Scott that reviews what safety features need to be in a home including the bathroom, stairway and ramps and the kitchen.

http://www.amputee-coalition.org/easyread/inmotion/jul_aug_08/homesafety-ez.html

Home Safety Tips: a Comprehensive Resource
Contains information to keep children and seniors safe inside and around the home. Includes tips to prevent fires and intruders from coming into a home, as well as ideas to keep your home safe when on vacation.

http://www.atlantictraining.com/safety-tips/home-safety-tips.php

Home Safety Tips for Seniors
Tips for general, kitchen, bathroom, and drug safety.

http://www.aplaceformom.com/senior-care-resources/articles/home-safety-tips-for-seniors

International Association for Child Safety
A network of child safety professionals and babyproofers that can assist with childproofing your home.

http://iafcs.org/

Maintaining a Safe Dementia-Friendly Home
The Canadian Safety Council's article includes tips to help keep occupants who have dementia safer in their homes.

https://canadasafetycouncil.org/campaigns/maintaining-safe-dementia-friendly-home

My Safe Home
An interactive audio and video virtual tour inside a home, room by room, to identify dangers, and discover features that prevent fires and keep the occupants safe.

http://www.mysafehome.org/

National Fire Protection Association
A broad list of topics are available to learn more about safe practices in the home to avoid a fire hazard.

http://www.nfpa.org/public-education/by-topic/safety-in-the-home

Rebuilding At Home
Safe at Home Checklist created in partnership with the Administration on Aging and the American Occupational Therapy Association

http://www.assistedlivingct.com/wp-content/uploads/2013/01/RT-Aging-in-Place-Safe-at-Home-Checklist.pdf

Universal Design Toolkit

Safety in the Home
A checklist to ensure safety for young children in the home, fire prevention and detection ideas, and burglar proofing a home.

http://www.realsimple.com/home-organizing/organizing/home-safety-checklist

Safety in the Home: Checklists
A collection of 41 safety checklists for inside a home and garage as well as outside in the landscape and play areas.

http://www.mortgagecalculator.org/helpful-advice/home-safety.php

Slip, Trip and Fall Prevention will Keep Older Adults Safe and Independent
The National Safety Council's article and checklist on suggestions to prevent falls for older adults.

http://www.nsc.org/learn/safety-knowledge/Pages/safety-at-home-falls.aspx

U.S. Consumer Product Safety Commission
A vast collection of bulletins, safety alerts and product updates on hazards to avoid in and around the home.

http://www.cpsc.gov/en/Safety-Education/Safety-Guides/Home/

Safety at Home: Adapting the home to support a person with dementia
The Alzheimer's Association created a safety checklist and suggestions to assist caregivers of people with dementia to make their lives safer in the home.

http://www.alz.org/documents/dsw/Safety_at_Home.pdf

Universal Design Toolkit

HOME ASSESSMENTS

Universal Design Checklists and SafeScore

These 10 checklists detail over 130 universal design features for homes including the interior pathways, kitchen, bathroom, parking area, and walkways. Use this assessment tool to determine the degree to which a home has universal design and safe features. A Universal Design SafeScore is the percentage of how universally-designed a space is for a wide range of users. The higher the Universal Design SafeScore, the greater the safety of the space assessed. This is due to design features that collectively minimize risk of injury for everyday activities.

http://www.safescore.org

CHECKLISTS

SURVEY FINDS HOMEBUYERS NEEDS FOR ACCESSIBLE HOUSING ARE UNMET

August 21, 2015

Source: Chicago Tribune

Research shows that the overwhelming majority of homebuyers with disabilities have a strong need and desire for real estate agents who are trained and knowledgeable about accessible housing options. But despite the need for adequate help, one in five homebuyers who have a disability say they do not get the proper assistance, according to a recent Century 21 Real Estate survey conducted by Harris Poll.

In a country where more than 54 million Americans live with disabilities, advocates across the nation recognize the importance of fostering inclusive communities that enable people with disabilities to live as fully integrated members of society. This includes helping people find accessible housing in the communities of their choice.

Organizations like Chicago-based Easter Seals and Access Living provide patrons with educational brochures, accessible home listings or housing counseling programs to ease the house-hunting process. But many homebuyers with disabilities still have trouble in their search, even with third-party help.

In recognition of the 25th anniversary of the Americans With Disabilities Act, Century 21 analyzed the current state of the real estate industry in relation to accessible housing. In its "Persons with Disabilities Home Buying Survey," the company looked at 503 U.S. adults interested in buying a home in the next three years. Participants either had disabilities or lived with someone who did.

Universal Design Toolkit

The findings offered stark evidence that despite real estate agents efforts to accommodate homebuyers with disabilities, the industry lacks the skills, tools and knowledge necessary to serve them. More than half the surveyed homebuyers rated real estate professionals knowledge of accessible housing at a C or below, and 49 percent of respondents said they have difficulty finding a home that fits their family's needs.

"We expected to see some of those results, but some of these numbers exceeded some of those expectations," said Mike Callaghan, Century 21s chief marketing officer.

The results confirmed there is a critical need to have real estate agents trained and educated "so they can better serve the unique needs of people with disabilities," Callaghan said. "(The findings) are somewhat of a call to action that real estate professionals have to do a better job for the families with disabilities."

Eighty-three percent of homebuyers with disabilities said they believe having a real estate agent who is knowledgeable about accessible housing would greatly benefit their house hunts, according to the survey.

Universal Design Toolkit

"If Realtors don't know (about accessible living) its not a deal breaker," said Easter Seals Chief Executive Randy Rutta. "But its a huge relief if they do. It makes you feel like you can make a better informed decision and that the person helping you make the biggest decision of your life understands who you are."

Rutta said each person with a disability faces a different challenge that affects his or her choice of a home. If the person is in a wheelchair, he needs to ask about mobility and physical accessibility to the house. If a couple has a child with a disability, they need to worry about finding an accommodating school in the area. If somebody can't drive, she needs to ensure the neighborhood provides accessible public transportation.

"Realtors are usually the first stop for consumers housing needs, so they are in a unique position to be strong advocates for greater accessibility for today's buyers," said Sara Wiskerchen, a spokeswoman for the National Association of Realtors. The trade groups At Home with Diversity course provides practical skills and tools for agents to better meet client's needs.

In response to the survey, Century 21 announced the development of a Special Agent Learning Program that will provide its agents with access to information and resources on accessible housing and universal design for people with disabilities.

Easter Seals, which has a long-standing relationship with Century 21, will provide the curriculum, content and resources necessary to develop the specific training as well as the materials that will give agents the gateway knowledge to better understand the needs of families with disabilities, Callaghan said.

"Its a complex situation, and the needs vary widely," he said, referring to the range of issues that affect people with disabilities, including blindness, deafness and lack of mobility. "I think because each of these needs is unique, its difficult to fully understand and provide counsel to these folks."

 Universal Design Toolkit

The optional training, which Century 21 will provide to its agents nationwide, will help agents understand how different homes can fit with different disabilities as well as provide them with the tools to find helpful community centers near the potential homes of families with disabilities. Century 21 will launch the program in October during its annual leadership conference in San Diego.

Although Rutta believes this is a viable first step to "making the presence of a disability as transparent as possible and as non-limiting as possible," he said there is still more work to be done in the housing industry in general. Affordable housing is difficult for people with disabilities to find. Architects, contractors and builders need to educate themselves about the importance of universal design so there can be a greater housing stock for people with disabilities.

"There was a lot of learning about the Americans with Disabilities Act and Fair Housing Act around 25 years ago, but it takes a while for people to really understand what that means," he said.

http://adasoutheast.org/news/articles.php?id=7910

15 PERCEIVED VALUE OF VISITABLE HOUSING IN OHIO - SUMMARY

This executive summary is from the study "**Perceived Value of Visitable Housing in Ohio**", authored by Jack L. Nasar, City & Regional Planning, The Ohio State University and Julia R. Elmer, City & Regional Planning, The Ohio State University.

A copy of the full report is available for download at:

http://ddc.ohio.gov/Portals/0/visitability-report-6-15.pdf

Executive Summary

A "visitable" house enables someone who has an ambulatory difficulty to enter and navigate the living area of the main floor of a residence. It has:

- One zero-step or low-slope entrance,
- Doorways at least 32" wide, and
- A usable half-bathroom on the first floor.

By 2024, it is estimated that Ohio may have 5 million residents with ambulatory difficulties. Houses with well-designed visitable features can benefit that population as well as injured veterans, the public, and the state. They can enhance independence and care-giving, lower costs incurred due to falls and injuries, lower Medicaid costs by allowing home care, and minimize tax expenditures by not requiring people to move to a nursing home or long-term care facility. However, developers complain about a lack of consumer demand for visitable units, stigma associated with visitable features, and higher costs associated with building such houses. Perhaps their perceptions are inaccurate or the perceived lack of consumer demand results from consumers seeing poorly designed visitable features or not seeing them at all.

Surveys of 266 Ohio homeowners, homebuyers, developers, and other real-estate professionals were conducted to learn more about the obstacles and benefits of visitable houses by showing respondents visitable features and asking them to respond to a range of questions. Results indicated:

- Strong consumer demand for visitable features;
- Low cost for providing features in new construction; and
- Improved livability associated with each feature.

To inform the design of the surveys, builders, real estate agents, and designers participated in discussions and focus groups (summarized in the Appendices). The on-line surveys with color photos of visitable and non-visitable features were taken by 266 Ohio residents (96 homeowners, 107 homebuyers, 39 builders, developers, and designers, and 24 real estate agents and appraisers).

Although most of the homeowners and homebuyers expected houses with a visitable feature to sell for more than houses without it, and although most of them believed that such a house was home to an older person or a wheelchair user, respondents:

- Preferred to buy the houses with a visitable feature; and
- Thought houses with visitable features would sell faster than houses lacking such features.

Builders, developers, and designers with experience with visitable houses estimated the cost in new construction as:

Universal Design Toolkit

- Less than one percent of the construction cost; and

- $3,180.00 less than the cost of retrofitting a house to make it visitable.

All three surveys found that each visitable feature improved livable qualities, such as:

- Access

- Aesthetics

- Resale value

- Ease of moving in or out or moving furniture

The benefits of visitable features to consumers and the state, their relative low cost, and consumer demand for them all suggest that Ohio can benefit from offering incentives to encourage the construction of visitable units.

16 RESOURCES

Listings are ordered by date, most recent publication first

"**Universal Design Guidelines for Homes in Ireland**", Centre for Excellence in Universal Design, 2015. Free download copies of several books with universal design guidelines and example floorplans.

http://universaldesign.ie/Built-Environment/Housing/

"**Human Factors in the Built Environment**", Linda L. Nussbaumer, Fairchild Books, 2014

"**Pure Style Home: Accessible Ideas for Every Room in your Home**", Jane Cumberbatch, Ryland Peters & Small, 2014

"**Universal Design Tips: Lessons Learned from Two UD Homes**", Ron Knecht & John Salmen, AIA, 2014

"**Modern Ideas, Modern Living: Taking the Next Step in Home Design and Planning for the Lifestyle You Want**", The Hartford Center for Mature Market Excellence, March 2013. Free download copy: http://www.thehartford.com/sites/thehartford/files/modern-ideas-2012.pdf

"**Simple Solutions: Practical Ideas and Products to Enhance Independent Living**", The Hartford Center for Mature Market Excellence, March 2013.

Free download copy: http://www.thehartford.com/sites/thehartford/files/simple-solutions-2012.pdf

"**Universal Design: Creating Inclusive Environments**", Edward Steinfeld and Jordana Maisel, Wiley, 2012

"**Universal Design as a Rehabilitation Strategy**", Jon A. Sanford, Springer Publishing Company, 2012

 Universal Design Toolkit

"**Inclusive Design: A Universal Need**", Linda L. Nussbaumer, Fairchild Books, 2012

"**Home Accessibility: 300 Tips for Making Life Easier**", Shelley Peterman Schwarz, Demos Health, 2012

"**Knack Universal Design: A Step-by-Step Guide to Modifying Your Home for Comfortable, Accessible Living**" (Knack: Make It Easy), Barbara Krueger and Nika Stewart, Knack, an Imprint of Globe Pequot Press, 2010

"**AARP Guide to Revitalizing Your Home: Beautiful Living for the Second Half of Life**", Rosemary Bakker, Lark, 2010

"**Universal Design Handbook, Second Edition**", Wolfgang Preiser and Korydon Smith, McGraw-Hill, 2010

"**Houses That Work for Life!**", Lisa Sandlin, Booksurge Publishing, 2009

"**Residential Design for Aging in Place**", Drew Lawlor and Michael A. Thomas, Wiley, 2008

"**Universal Design for the Home: Great-Looking, Great-Living Design for All Ages, Abilities, and Circumstances**", Wendy A. Jordan, Quarry Books, 2008

"**Universal and Accessible Design for Products, Services, and Processes**", Robert F. Erlandson, CRC Press, 2008

"**Installing Trench Drains in Curbless Showers**", The Center for Universal Design, North Carolina State University, 2007

    https://www.ncsu.edu/www/ncsu/design/sod5/cud/pubs_p/docs/trench_drain.pdf

Universal Design Toolkit

"**Creating Stepless Entrances in Multifamily Housing**", The Center for Universal Design, North Carolina State University, 2007

> https://www.ncsu.edu/www/ncsu/design/sod5/cud/pubs_p/docs/Stepless_Entrances.pdf

"**Universal Design and Visitability: From Accessibility to Zoning**", Jack Nasar & Jennifer Evans-Cowley, The John Glenn School of Public Affairs, 2007

"**Universal Design Ideas for Style, Comfort & Safety**", RSMeans and Lexicon Consulting Inc., 2007

"**Residential Rehabilitation, Remodeling and Universal Design**", The Center for Universal Design, North Carolina State University, 2006

> https://www.ncsu.edu/www/ncsu/design/sod5/cud/pubs_p/docs/residential_remodelinl.pdf

"**Accessible Home Design: Architectural Solutions for the Wheelchair User**" Second Edition, Thomas D. Davies and Carol Peredo Lopez, Paralyzed Veterans of America Distribution Center, 2006

"**Home Planning for Your Later Years**" William K. Wasch, Beverly Cracom Publications, 2006

"**Remodeling for Easy Access Living**", Rick Peters, Popular Mechanics, 2006

"**Universal Design "Smart" Homes for the 21st Century: 102 Home Plans You Can Order and Build**", Charles Schwab, Schwab Publishers, 2005

"**The Right Space: A Wheelchair Accessibility Guide for Single-Family Homes**", Albert Ayala, Debold-Marquez Books, LLC, 2005

 Universal Design Toolkit

"**Bathroom Options for Multifamily Housing in North Carolina**", The Center for Universal Design, North Carolina State University, 2005

https://www.ncsu.edu/www/ncsu/design/sod5/cud/pubs_p/docs/qap_tech_screen.pdf

"**Directory of Accessible Building Products**", NAHB Research Center, 2005

"**Using Your Home to Stay at Home**", National Council on Aging, 2004

"**We the People: Aging in the United States**", Census 2000 Special Reports, Issued December 2004

"**Universal Design Features in Houses: Gold, Silver, Bronze**", The Center for Universal Design, North Carolina State University, 2004

https://www.ncsu.edu/www/ncsu/design/sod5/cud/pubs_p/docs/GBS.pdf

"**AARP Beyond 50.03**", A Report to the Nation on Independence and Disability, AARP, 2003

"**Curbless Showers: An Installation Guide**", The Center for Universal Design, North Carolina State University, 2003

https://www.ncsu.edu/www/ncsu/design/sod5/cud/pubs_p/docs/Curbless.pdf

"**The Accessible Home: Updating Your Home for Changing Physical Needs**", Creative Publishing International, 2003

"**High Access Home: Design and Decoration for Barrier-Free Living**", Charles A. Iii Riley, Rizzoli Universe Promotional Books, 2003

"**Living Independently in Your Later Years**", A special report of the Harvard Medical School, Harvard Health Publications, 2002

Universal Design Toolkit

"**Aging in Place- Solutions to a Crisis in Housing and Care**", Neighborhood Reinvestment Corporation, August 2002

"**A Quiet Crisis in America**", The Report to Congress by the Commission on Affordable Housing and Health Facility Needs for Seniors in the 21st Century, June 30, 2002

"**Universal Design**", Selwyn Goldsmith, Architectural Press, 2001

"**A Basic Guide to Fair Housing Accessibility: Everything Architects and Builders Need to Know About the Fair Housing Act Accessibility Guidelines**", Steven Winter Associates, Inc., John Wiley & Sons, 2001

"**Universal Design Handbook**", Wolfgang Preiser and Elaine Ostroff, Editors; McGraw-Hill, 2001

"**Aging in Place, Coordinating Housing and Health Care Provision for America's Growing Elderly Population**", The Harvard University Joint Center on Housing Studies in conjunction with the Neighborhood Reinvestment Corporation report entitled, October 2001

"**Aging in Place – Aging and the Impact of Interior Design**", American Society of Interior Designers, 2001

"**Products and Plans for Universal Homes**", Home Planners, LLC, 2000

"**Fixing to Stay**", A National Survey of Housing and Home Modification Issues, AARP, May 2000

"**Aging in Place**", Ellen D. Taira and Jodi L. Carlson, Editors, The Haworth Press, Inc., 1999

"**High-Access Home: Design and Decoration for Barrier-Free Living**", Charles A. Riley II, Ph.D., Rizzoli, 1999

"**Universal Interiors by Design: Gracious Spaces**", Mary Jo Peterson and Irma Dobkin, McGraw-Hill, 1999

Universal Design Toolkit

"**Beautiful Universal Design: A Visual Guide**", Cynthia Leibrock, James Terry, James Evan Terry, Wiley John & Sons, 1999

"**The Universal Design File: Designing for People of All Ages and Abilities**", Molly Story, James Mueller, Ronald Mace, The Center for Universal Design, 1998

"**Universal Kitchen and Bathroom Planning: Design That Adapts to People**", Mary Jo Peterson, McGraw-Hill Professional Publishing, 1998

"**Universal Design: Creative Solutions for ADA Compliance**", Roberta L. Null, Professional Publications Inc, 1998

"**Fair Housing Act Design Manual**", Barrier Free Environments, Inc., 1998

"**Principles of Universal Design**", The Center for Universal Design, North Carolina State University, 1997

> https://www.ncsu.edu/www/ncsu/design/sod5/cud/about_ud/udprinciples.htm

"**Accessible Housing by Design: Universal Design Principles in Practice**", Steven Winter Associates, McGraw-Hill, 1997

"**Elder Design: Designing and Furnishing a Home for Your Later Years**", Rosemary Bakker, Penguin Group, 1997

"**Residential Remodeling and Universal Design: Making Homes More Comfortable and Accessible**", U. S. Department of Housing and Urban Development, 1996

"**Accessible Housing**", Leon A. Frechette, McGraw-Hill, 1996

"**Emerging Technologies for Independent Living**", The Center for Universal Design, North Carolina State University, 1995

> https://www.ncsu.edu/www/ncsu/design/sod5/cud/pubs_p/pemergtech.htm

 Universal Design Toolkit

"**Building for a Lifetime: The Design and Construction of Fully Accessible Homes**", Margaret Wylde, Adrian Baron-Robbins and Sam Clark, Taunton Press, 1994

"**Enabling Garden: Creating Barrier-free Gardens**", Gene Rothert, Taylor Publishing Co., 1994

"**The Accessible Housing Design File**", Barrier Free Environments, Inc., John Wiley & Sons, 1991

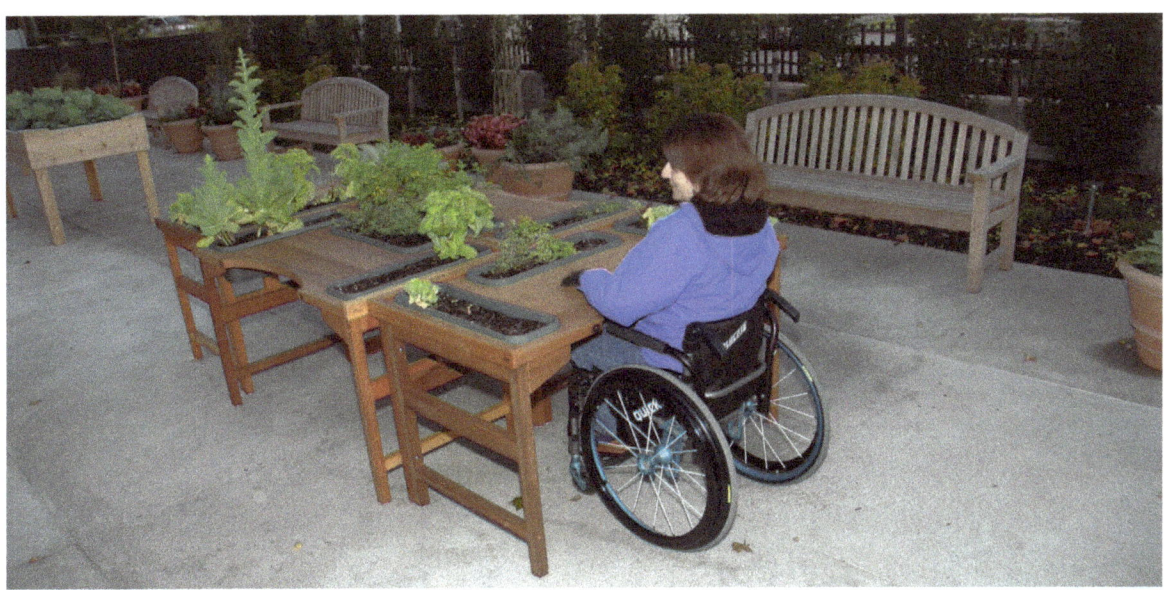

RESOURCES: Fair Housing Act

- Fair Housing Information Clearinghouse
  http://fhic.nfhta.org

- National Fair Housing Alliance
  http://www.nationalfairhousing.org

- **U.S. Department of Housing and Urban Development**

  - General Information
    http://www.hud.gov/fairhousing
    Hotline: 800-669-9777

Universal Design Toolkit

- <http://www.hud.gov>

- Fair Housing Accessibility Guidelines
  <http://portal.hud.gov/hudportal/HUD?src=/program_offices/fair_housing_equal_opp/disabilities/fhefhag>

- Fair Housing and Equal Opportunity
  <http://portal.hud.gov/hudportal/HUD?src=/program_offices/fair_housing_equal_opp>

- Fair Housing Laws and Presidential Executive Orders
  <http://portal.hud.gov/hudportal/HUD?src=/program_offices/fair_housing_equal_opp/FHLaws>

- U.S. Department of Justice
  <https://www.justice.gov/>

RESOURCES: Americans with Disabilities Act

- ADA Accessibility Guidelines (ADAAG)
  <https://www.access-board.gov/guidelines-and-standards/buildings-and-sites/about-the-ada-standards/background/adaag>

- ADA Basic Building Blocks Course
  <http://www.adabasics.org/>

- ADA Best Practices Tool Kit for State and Local Governments
  <https://www.ada.gov/pcatoolkit/abouttoolkit.htm>

- ADA Checklist for Readily Achievable Barrier Removal
  <https://www.ada.gov/checkweb.htm>

- Mid-Atlantic ADA Center
  <http://www.adainfo.org/>

- ADA Library
  <http://askjan.org/links/adalinks.htm>

 Universal Design Toolkit

- ADA National Network
  http://www.adagame.org/

- U.S. Access Board
  https://www.access-board.gov/

RESOURCES: Architectural Barriers Act

- Architectural Barriers Act of 1968, U.S. Access Board
  https://www.access-board.gov/the-board/laws/architectural-barriers-act-aba

RESOURCES: Section 504 of the Rehabilitation Act

- **U.S. Department of Housing and Urban Development**

  - Section 504 One-Stop Web Site
    http://portal.hud.gov/hudportal/HUD?src=/program_offices/fair_housing_equal_opp/disabilities/sect504

  - Section 504 of the Rehabilitation Act of 1973
    http://portal.hud.gov/hudportal/HUD?src=/programdescription/sec504

ABOUT ROSEMARIE ROSSETTI, PH.D.

Rich Sharick / Rich Images Photography

Rosemarie Rossetti, Ph.D. is a powerful, internationally known speaker, consultant, writer, and publisher who walks her talk. As a professional speaker and member of the National Speakers Association, she speaks from experience.

She has her Ph.D. and M.S. degrees in Agricultural Education from The Ohio State University, where she also earned her B.S. degree with dual major in Agricultural Education and Horticulture.

She was on the faculty at The Ohio State University from 1986-1997 where she taught courses in public speaking and teaching methods.

She established Rossetti Enterprises Inc. in 1997, and is the president.

On June 13, 1998 Rossetti sustained a spinal cord injury when a 3-1/2 ton tree fell on her while she was riding her bicycle. This life changing catastrophe led to her personal journey of recovery and a new focus for her speaking business.

Rossetti and her husband, Mark Leder are the owners, occupants and builders of the Universal Design Living Laboratory, the national demonstration home and garden in Columbus, Ohio. This is the highest rated universal design home in North America earning three national certifications. The home achieved a Silver LEED rating, and a Gold rating on the National Green Building Standard certification program. Their home has received 10 national certifications, commendations and

 Universal Design Toolkit

tributes. To see articles, photos, videos, contributors, webinars, and take a virtual tour go to: www.udll.com

Rossetti is a keynote and breakout session speaker at national conferences, speaking about universal design and green building. To view the description and learning outcomes of her presentation, *Designing & Building Sustainable Homes that Make Life Easier* and read testimonial letters, go to: http://www.udll.com/programs-services/designing-and-building-sustainable-homes-that-make-life-easier/

Rossetti and Leder's presentations help people integrate universal design and green building features into their projects. They consult with architects, developers, builders, remodelers, Realtors, interior designers, and consumers who are building or remodeling homes in order to design them with universal design and green features. They have earned the Certified Living in Place Professional™ designation. They work with building and design professionals that want to create inspired and livable homes.

Rossetti is also a motivational speaker who helps people cope with change and deal with adversity. She speaks to organizations and corporations that want to bring out the best in people and demonstrates how to live life with conviction. To view a description of her program *Just Like Riding a Bike* and see her bio, client list, program descriptions, articles, testimonials and videos go to www.RosemarieSpeaks.com

She is the author of the book "Take Back Your Life!", where she revealed the lessons she learned and lived by after her spinal cord injury.

Rossetti's *Accessible Home* monthly column was published from March 2006 – June 2011 in Action Magazine, a national publication of the United Spinal Association. Her articles about designing homes have appeared in: Ultimate Home Design, 50+ magazine, Best in American Living, PN magazine, Special Living Magazine, Columbus Monthly, and Ability Magazine. Rossetti's chapter on the Universal Design Living Laboratory is included in the second edition of the Universal Design Handbook.

Universal Design Toolkit

Rossetti was a member of the AARP national coalition on universal design. She was a member of the Ohio Visitability Strategy Group to improve the availability of accessible and visitable homes in Ohio.

Rossetti created and delivered her universal design and green building, day long, course nationwide in eleven major cities from March 2010 to April 2011. *Designing Sustainable Homes that Make Life Easier* was accredited for architects and interior designers.

Rossetti was certified as a course instructor for the National Association of Home Builder's Universal Design/Build course. She was a presenter in 2006 at their International Builders Show and at their 50+ Housing Symposium.

Rossetti's radio interviews on universal design have been featured on Blog Talk Radio, and Builder Radio. She has delivered webinars for the National Association of REALTORS®, National Association of the Remodeling Industry, and GreenHome Institute.

The Columbus REALTORS® presented Rossetti with the Instructor of the Year Award in 2016. Other honors include: Unsung Hero Humanitarian Award, 2014; National "Roll Model" Discovery through Design Fashion Show, 2007; Ms. Wheelchair Ohio 2004; Winter Olympic Torchbearer, 2002.

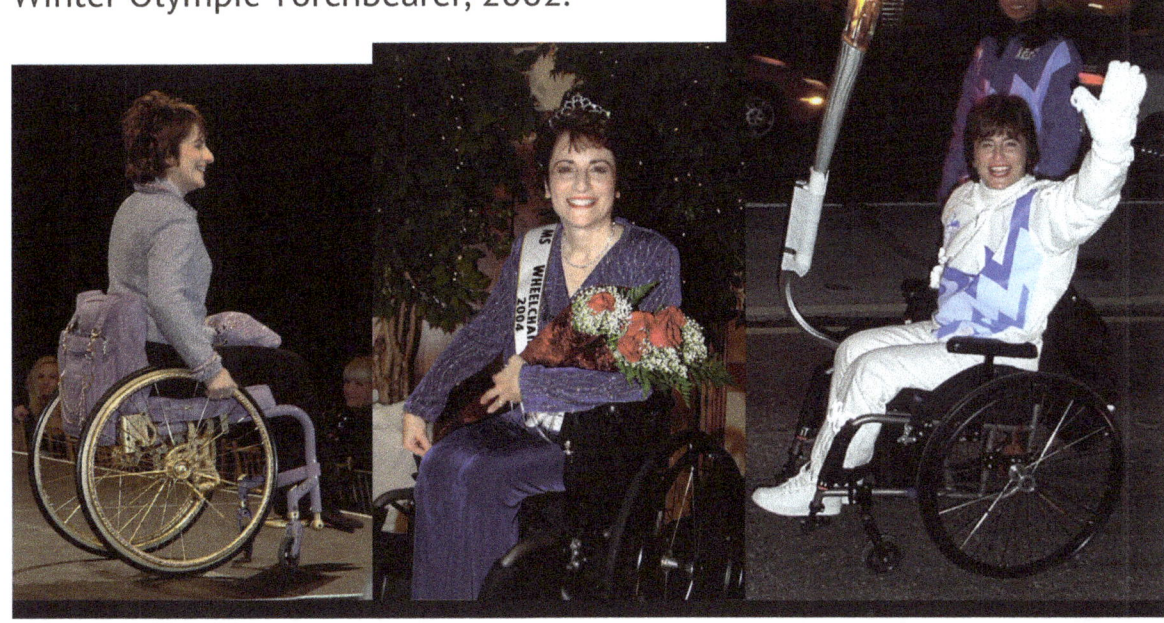

ABOUT ROSEMARIE

PUTTING UNIVERSAL DESIGN TO WORK FOR YOU

Consulting

Mark Leder and Rosemarie Rossetti, Ph.D. are available to consult with you, and your design team or client. They will work on a single family home plan or on a larger residential development project. If convenient, they can meet with you by appointment in their home, the Universal Design Living Laboratory, in Columbus, Ohio. Another option for people not able to travel to Columbus, they can discuss the project on the phone, or through video chats on the Internet. House plans can be sent electronically, or delivered to their home. Each project is customized based on the client's needs. Fees will be discussed when the scope of the project is determined.

 Universal Design Toolkit

Presentations

They can also be hired to deliver presentations about universal design and green building throughout the U.S. as well as internationally. Programs can be as short as 30 minutes or six hours in one day.

To learn more about Rosemarie, visit her speaking business website at www.RosemarieSpeaks.com In addition to speaking about universal design and green building, she is also a motivational speaker who speaks about coping with change and dealing with adversity.

To hire them, please contact:

- Rosemarie Rossetti, Ph.D. Rosemarie@udll.com
- Mark Leder Mark@udll.com

To order additional copies of "The Universal Design Toolkit", please visit:

http://www.universaldesigntoolkit.com/reorder

www.ingramcontent.com/pod-product-compliance
Lightning Source LLC
Chambersburg PA
CBHW061142010526
44118CB00026B/2842